Tracing Paradise

Tracing Paradise

Two Years in Harmony
with John Milton

A Reader's Memoir

Dawn Potter

University of Massachusetts Press
Amherst

LC 2009010156
ISBN 978-1-55849-701-6
Designed by Jack Harrison
Set in Adobe Jenson Pro
Printed and bound by The Maple-Vail Book Manufacturing Group
Library of Congress Cataloging-in-Publication Data

Potter, Dawn, 1964–
Tracing Paradise : two years in harmony with John Milton : a reader's memoir /
Dawn Potter.
p. cm.
Includes bibliographical references.
ISBN 978-1-55849-701-6 (pbk. : alk. paper)
1. Potter, Dawn, 1964– 2. Poets, American—20th century—Biography.
3. Milton, John, 1608–1674. Paradise lost. 4. Poetry—Authorship. I. Title.
PS3616.O8485Z46 2009
811'.6—dc22
[B]
2009010156

British Library Cataloguing in Publication data are available.

Frontispiece: Jonathan Fisher, *Forlorn Maiden,* c. 1825, woodblock print, 2 x 2 ⁹/₁₆ ".
Farnsworth Art Museum, Gift of Mr. Frank H. Teagle, Jr., 1967.

for Baron

What a thing it is to grasp the nature of the whole firmament and of its stars. . . . Besides this, what delight it affords to the mind to take its flight through the history and geography of every nation and to observe the changes in the conditions of kingdoms, races, cities, and peoples, to the increase of wisdom and righteousness. This, my hearers, is to live in every period of the world's history, and to be as it were coeval with time itself.

—JOHN MILTON, Prolusion VII (circa 1632)

Contents

Acknowledgments

This book exists because my friend Baron Wormser told me to write it. After that alarming pronouncement, he then followed through by reading the first draft of every chapter. His skill, affection, and intellectual impatience are tonic.

Thanks to George Core at the *Sewanee Review*, Wendy Lesser at the *Threepenny Review*, and Willard Spiegelman at the *Southwest Review* for publishing early versions of several chapters and for igniting a continued epistolary friendship. Susan Danly, curator of graphics, photography, and contemporary art at the Portland Museum of Art; Bethany Engstrom, assistant registrar at the Farnsworth Museum; and my husband, photographer Thomas Birtwistle, dealt quickly and elegantly with my last-minute illustration quandaries. I'm grateful as well for the skill and encouragement of Bruce Wilcox, Carol Betsch, and Jack Harrison at the press and freelance editor Kay Scheuer, and for the very helpful advice of Rachel Hadas and Sam Pickering. Finally, and especially, I thank Steve Cayard, not only for his practical assistance in the matter of my goat but for his conversation, his generosity, and his kindness.

Tracing Paradise

1
Chores

On heav'nly ground they stood, and from the shore
They view'd the vast immeasurable Abyss
Outrageous as a Sea, dark, wasteful, wild,
Up from the bottom turn'd by furious winds
And surging waves, as Mountains to assault
Heav'n's highth, and with the Centre mix the Pole.

A<small>T SOME JUNCTURE</small> of nearly every morning, I copy out a few lines of Milton's *Paradise Lost*. I type my day's dose on a small laptop computer perched on a foldout shelf in the study corner of my bedroom, a jumbly combination of the beautiful and the half-baked: the lovely crammed inset bookcases built by my husband Tom and the temporary (for ten years or so) clamp-lamp lighting we haven't gotten around to replacing; the elegant antique cherry writing table his parents bought us when we had no furniture and the cheesy fake-Persian rug I got on sale at Reny's, a tiny department store with unpredictable merchandise, located in Dexter, fifteen miles down a frost-heaved road from our house in Harmony,

Maine. Over my desk are tacked postcards of Caravaggio paintings, a grubby needlepoint eggplant I laboriously stitched when I was eight, a picture ripped out of *Mojo* showing Mick Jagger in a frilly shirt reciting Shelley's *Adonais* at Brian Jones's funeral ("'Tis we who lost in stormy visions keep / With phantoms an unprofitable strife"), a scrap of raw pine board with my name spelled out in nail holes (a birthday gift from my hammer-happy son James). It's a lovely place to work, and once two moose in a breeding frenzy burst out of the forest right below my window, which adds to the corner's aura of accomplishment.

But before I can rendezvous with Milton, I have to talk myself into getting out of bed. On a usual winter morning that means forcing myself away from a warm husband into the pitch-dark of 5:30 A.M., down a flight of steep stairs from our attic bedroom, down into a house that for some hours now has been rapidly chilling.

It's easy to be histrionic about the difficulties of getting out of bed, and a cold climate makes the melodrama even easier. According to Norse myth, life began when the frost giant Ymir and his ice cow exploded from a vacant pit trapped between a land of frozen fog and one of roaring fire. In Maine, this version of creation can, at certain seasons, seem perfectly plausible; and if I'd been the author of *Paradise Lost*, I might have imagined hell as a barren fortress of wind and sleet. For there comes a time in every year when all work in the house takes second place to fire; and I am the unskilled fire-starter who is, on most mornings, responsible for kindling the spark.

If you live in a house with central heating, it's easy to believe that warmth is an inalienable right, that humanity has reduced its epic struggle with the elements to an irritating spat with a draughty window or a damp sock. A hurricane or a tsunami may hurl us temporarily back into Milton's world; but like all animals, we live in the present tense. What happens in front of our eyes seems truer than anything else.

In front of me every morning is a black iron maw that must be fed paper and kindling and split maple. And this is just the end of the story; there's the Little Red Hen litany that has led me to the moment of lighting a match. Who will choose the trees to cut? Who will sharpen the chainsaw? Who will haul the logs into the dooryard? Who will split them into firewood? Who will stack them in the woodshed? Who will carry them into the house?

> Is this the Region, this the Soil, the Clime,
> Said then the lost Arch-Angel, this the seat
> That we must change for Heav'n, this mournful gloom
> For that celestial light?[1]

Like a string of beads or a game of cards, a chore has a history. One task follows the next, follows the next. There's pattern and tedium and necessity and skill. You learn exactly how to balance six split logs on your left arm, how to shift your load and flatten your step when you cross a patch of ice, how to tip your armload smoothly into the woodbox. You learn how to talk yourself into and out of laziness. You learn there are some chores you'll never be much good at. You learn you have to do them anyway.

I am not much good at starting fires. After a dozen years on the job, I still catch myself stuffing paper, kindling, and logs into the firebox in the wrong order. Some days I forget to close or open drafts or dampers and either smother the flame or fill the room with smoke. There are mornings when I kneel on the hearthrug in despair, watching one match after another flare up pettishly and then choke to death. Despair is not too strong a word when you can't manage to heat your house.

Eavesdropping on Adam and Eve's embraces, the Fiend soliloquizes:

> Live while ye may,
> Yet happy pair; enjoy, till I return,
> Short pleasures, for long woes are to succeed.[2]

And thank heaven for those short pleasures, for there is no solace like a lover who also knows how to rescue a fire on a dark January morning. Criticizers incessantly scold Milton for describing the pair's marital balance of power as "Hee for God only, shee for God in him," but isn't that just another way of acknowledging the value of both a private life and a bond of grateful affection? Our manners and mores have evolved insofar as we can now interchange the pronouns as easily we interchange our familial actions. The ideal itself remains.[3]

Managing to light the woodstove, rushing to brew coffee and carry up a cup to Tom as impetus to hoist himself out of bed, slicing bread and ham for school lunches, sorting my sons' dirty shirts: all these chores may look like docile "shee for God in him" tasks, and indeed they are; for if I can't see God in the ones I love, where can God be? But at the same time, when I do my work, I "am for God only," for the tasks are a song of myself, the daily story of my hands and eyes, my talents and errors. They are a secret ritual, a hair shirt, a burden, a shield, a gift with no reward but itself.

> Then shall this mount
> Of Paradise by might of Waves be mov'd
> Out of his place, push'd by the horned flood,
> With all his verdure spoil'd, and Trees adrift
> Down the great River to the op'ning Gulf,
> And there take root an Island salt and bare,
> The haunt of Seals and Orcs, and Sea-mews' clang.
> To teach thee that God attributes to place
> No sanctity, if none be thither brought
> By Men who there frequent, or therein dwell.[4]

Reading is a subset of living, and food and heat are more important than words. One might argue, then, that Eve's allotted task was more essential than Adam's. But I think that's beside the point. Both portions are their own burden, their own release. And in the history of my days, which in large part have turned out to be an amalgam of tending home and tending words, reading is a particular gift: it's one of the few things I can save for later because it doesn't need to be fed or watered or mucked out. While I light a match or knead dough, *Paradise Lost* sits safely in the vault, like a dragon asleep on a heap of coins.

Milton isn't the only dragon in my vault. But for nearly two years now, he's been king, with the rest of my usual dragons shrinking to salamander-size. And he's been a curious addition to my savings, for until this point I would never have claimed *Paradise Lost* as a guide. I would have been more likely to classify it as one of several routine tortures inflicted by high school English teachers on sensitive and romantic young girls who would rather be mooning over the sonnets of Keats.

But then I couldn't abide Tom, that skinny, silent, sarcastic votary of loud music, until I fell in love with him. Difficulty wasn't the point; for many a romantic and sensitive young girl adores a bad boy who treats her mean, who tromps on her ideals, who has no interest in conciliation and ignores her tears. Perhaps it was the poem's emotional unreality, for despite its chronologically young lovers, *Paradise Lost* is a middle-aged romance, concerned with duty far more than ecstasy.

I've always enjoyed thinking of myself as a romantic and sensitive young girl, though time is rubbing that lie thin, and housework has as well. I look at my forty-year-old hands, and I think, "Well, look! They're capable!" It's a surprise, a rueful pleasure, to cast off the pale delicacies of girlhood and admit, instead, to a calloused pride in getting it done, whether "it" be stacking firewood, or beating dough, or digging potatoes, or scrubbing a sink. All this sounds Wendell Berry-ish in the extreme, but I don't make a claim for any political commitment to self-reliance. As my friend Steve told me one night at a party, "Before enlightenment I hauled water and chopped wood. And after enlightenment I hauled water and chopped wood." Here we are, and we're making do.

Paradise Lost is, among many other things, a poem about making do. And this was a surprise to me, for I undertook my project to copy out all of *Paradise Lost* after convincing myself it was time to start seriously studying great works that were antithetical to me in some inner personal way. While I've always been a voracious reader, I tend to cling to certain poems and novels because I sense they've saved a special place for me. I expect this is a simplistic view of the draw of books, yet I think it's common enough among a certain sort of literary nonacademic. V. S. Naipaul immersed himself in the work of Dickens, and so did I, many years younger and many degrees colder. So did Henry James, older and stodgier than both of us. So did the character Captain Brown in Elizabeth Gaskell's *Cranford*, who gets run over by a train while reading *The Pickwick Papers*. I could have been crossing that track.

It has never seemed likely, however, that I'd be run over by a train while reading *Paradise Lost*. I've always been suspicious of its motives—too moral, too stiff; caring too much about grandeur, not enough about the pokey little accidents of living; like putting on a scratchy ruffed collar every day but never being allowed to take a bath. And yet here I am, discovering line after line that John Milton speaks the language of my heart—possibly a heart I didn't know I had, possibly a heart I didn't know he had . . . in either case, a small treasure I've begun slowly to unwrap, when I have time, when I'm not making do, when I am making do. For the poem has become a sort of pattern for me, a sort of fascination. It's so puzzling and so plain, so far and so close, so boring and so mesmerizing. It's so brave. He's not afraid to be grandiose and bossy. Nor is he afraid to ponder exactly how an angel's digestive system might work. Nor is he afraid to admit that it really would be a pleasure to sit chit-chatting over lunch with Adam and Raphael, all three of them watching naked Eve bustle around pouring wine. He admits this sounds libidinous. But wouldn't it be wonderful if it there were some intermediate stage between lust and cool admiration?

Milton is full of such hopeful regrets, and many of them center around household affairs. For in his mind, marriage equals work. Eve doesn't lie around like an odalisque all day: "to the Field they haste." She and Adam prune branches and pick fruit. They gather supplies for dinner; they devise places to sit and sleep. The sun burns at noonday, and they get hot and tired. When the angel Raphael comes to visit, Eve, "with dispatchful looks in haste / She turns, on hospitable thoughts intent," crushing grapes, "temper[ing] dulcet creams." Even in Eden, they go into a tizzy over unexpected guests. Clearly, in Milton's terms, paradise isn't indolence. It's sharing a common responsibility. And to me the important point here is "in Milton's terms." For *Paradise Lost* is very much a private lament.[5]

This, as much as anything, accounts for my present fascination with the poem; and I've only tripped over such surprises (for the poem is constantly surprising) by having, somewhat accidentally, made a habit of copying it word for word. Though I took on the project as a kind of forced self-improvement, a way of shoehorning myself into a deeper knowledge of poetic craft, I never really believed I'd stick with the job. I often copy out shorter poems as a way of immersing myself in details of syntax, line, grammar, punctuation, rhythm, suspense . . . all those quirks so particular to how poets fashion their poems. But *Paradise Lost* is twelve books long, with more than ten thousand lines. Twelve gnarled, moth-eaten, proto-Christian, antifeminist books packed with archaic sentence structure and italicized classical allusions! Twelve soporific books devoted ad nauseam to the dull adventures of cardboard biblical action figures! Twelve solemn, self-satisfied books littered with unpredictable capitalization and more show-off similes than Sylvia Plath could have dreamed up in an opium stupor! I had no intention of copying the whole thing. Possibly a few pages would be good enough.

Admitting my preconceived weakness in this regard is embarrassing. But it was just as embarrassing to tell other people that I had undertaken such a project, even in its original lily-livered form. Copying out *Paradise Lost* is not a way to impress people. For instance, I daresay most scholars of the poem would laugh at the notion, and I can understand why. Not being poets themselves, they don't need to dig their hands into the mud, so to speak; the physical stuff of the poem isn't their métier. But it was unnerving to discover that other poets also seemed to be stymied by the project. Except as a dramatic demonstration of "Oh, look how obsessive I am," they didn't see the point. If I sheepishly mentioned it during a class or a workshop, dutiful students sometimes took brief notes about the enterprise. (I imagine something along the lines of "Milton?") Most sat open-mouthed, in the classic fly-swallowing posture, though not from amazement. I'd say it was more like adenoidal uncertainty. It was unclear to me if they'd ever heard of Milton. Teachers tended to nod knowingly, possibly because they'd once taken notes on Milton themselves ("Great Chain of Being!" "Epic Simile!").

Probably, for all these people, reading *Paradise Lost* would indeed be useless. If nothing else, my relationship with this poem has reinforced my feeling that books are manic love affairs between reader and writer; and my pleasure in the poem has evolved into the strange comfort of habit. Often that means forcing myself by internal fiat to sit down at my desk and tap out two lines—just two lines—expecting and receiving nothing but aggravation. Some days it means racing through four pages, whipped up with excitement, and then running downstairs and blathering to Tom about my thrilling new image of God, "reaping [his] immortal fruits of joy and love," as sweet Victorian heroine.[6]

What *Paradise Lost* has become is housework. I don't love putting on my smelly coat every day and hiking into the cold to rinse chicken shit out of a frozen water dish. I don't love pounding not-dry-enough-to-burn-but-we're-out-of-the-good-stuff firewood from a frozen pile. I don't love italicizing an endless litany of unintelligible words like *Naptha* and *Asphaltus*, which Milton apparently plucked from the graveyard of classical antiquity just so he could show me how smart he is, though meanwhile I feel as if I've been deposited in a fifties A&P store and have no idea what he's talking about.

But I do love the accidents of happiness that accrue from those mornings spent among chilblains and splinters: the exceeding beauty of a golden sebright hen standing on one blue leg in the frosty sunlight, the cache of pale mushrooms a squirrel has tucked away among the birch logs, a poodle skating ineptly across an icy puddle. I do love to type out, slowly and with all capital letters and apostrophes intact, the promise that "neither do the Spirits damn'd / Lose all thir virtue." If that's not a comfort, what is?[7]

2

Stumbling into Harmony

Thus was this place,
A happy rural seat of various view.

Perhaps one definition of paradise is that it's a place that doesn't dash your hopes. I arrived in Harmony when I was twenty-eight, newly married, newly unemployed, eager to find my place on earth. I came to the north country prepared to be happy, and I *was* happy.

In this era of aimless migration and faceless commercial land-scape, finding a real home on earth is a miracle. Yet any attempt to explain its succor risks transforming the homebody into a mouth-piece for provincial nostalgics or back-to-the-land politicos. For it's very hard to explain a marriage, human or otherwise; and loving a place is like loving a husband or a cow or a baby or a grandfather: you make the best of it, you lose your temper, you throw up your hands in despair, you spin foolishly in circles, you take what's been served, and you shut up.

There's nothing charming about Harmony. It squats in the middle of the state, far away from the ocean, far away from the ski lodges. It has no scenic New England charm: its school is ugly, its town office uglier. It has a rundown yarn factory that once appeared in a Stephen King movie. It also has plenty of gas pumps and three places to buy beer. During hunting season you can tag your buck here very easily. Any time of the year you can buy bar-and-chain oil for your chainsaw. If you drive a half-hour south, you can shop at Wal-Mart. If you drive an hour east, you can go to the mall.

Clearly Harmony is not Brigadoon. Time has not forgotten us. This is a town that takes diesel seriously. Almost everyone watches a lot of TV and votes Republican. Junked pickups rust in the weeds, little children are horrifyingly fat, and men beat their wives. Mobile homes burn down. Trash piles up in the ditches. In my son's seventh-grade class, one very nice Christian boy recently suggested it might be a good idea to shoot all Mexicans who cross the U.S. border.

I realize that, at this point in my description, Harmony sounds like the town a *Harper's* writer might conjure up as an emblem of backcountry rot, a dying hamlet cretinously sponging up the poisons of our time. Hell, in fact. But hell is not always hell. As Satan notes,

> What when we fled amain, pursu'd and strook
> With Heav'n's afflicting Thunder, and besought
> The Deep to shelter us? this Hell then seem'd
> A refuge from those wounds.[1]

Thomas Hardy once wrote that "melancholy among the rural poor arises primarily from a sense of incertitude and precariousness of the position." And for the maimed, the scared, the defeated, the angry, the vengeful, a bleak backcountry can indeed be a place to lick your wounds, to ponder, to squirrel away the canned goods and the ammo. By a long shot, this doesn't make it Eden; but Milton's image of hell as refuge does offer some hint about the mutability of place in the human psyche. Like most overquoted lines, "The mind is its own place, and in itself / Can make a Heav'n of Hell, a Hell of Heav'n" resonates because it strikes a familiar knell: because we are alone and changeable in all our colors and seasons; because we and our refuge are one and the same.[2]

I didn't come to Harmony to lick my wounds. Since my only wounds were writing frustration and job anomie, I arrived here very nearly baggage-free, despite the cranky, bawling truckload of goats we'd hauled up with us. Those goats, as much as anything, were the impetus for moving here. For six years I'd been living in Rhode Island, rushing out of Providence to a friend's farm—twice every day, dawn and dusk—to wash udders, strip teats, strain milk, clean up afterbirth, bottle-feed kids. As board payment, I spent weekends in my friend's barn scraping out stalls and trimming hooves. I missed work for humiliating reasons. (Try saying to a textbook publisher, "Excuse me, my goat's in heat. Can I take the day off to get her bred?") I was living a double life between other people's borders, and in some inarticulate way I saw myself as a ghost who hadn't properly crossed over into the underworld but was doomed to flit among the made-for-somebody-else episodes of modern existence.

As the child of agrarian refugees who had themselves crossed over into the alien suburban world of the professional intellectual, I grew up fully conscious of the gravitational lure of the provinces; the backward glance; the poignant, helpless, regressive regret for burnt bridges and torched fields; the ancestors left lonely in the dooryard. It was baggage, as all childhoods are baggage, but it didn't necessarily influence my decision to escape to the north. Youth has a gift for fixing blame on whatever handy concrete catchphrase conveniently presents itself, and in my case, "no money," "no barn," and "got to get away" were reason enough.

But "got to get away" will only get you so far. Every time you get away, you arrive somewhere else. Unless you die in the saddle, you eventually have to make do with where you've landed. Sometimes making do means making peace. Sometimes it means stockpiling ammo.

> What if the breath that kindl'd those grim fires
> Awak'd should blow them into sevenfold rage
> And plunge us in the flames? or from above
> Should intermitted vengeance arm again
> His red right hand to plague us? what if all
> Her stores were op'n'd, and this Firmament
> Of Hell should spout her Cataracts of Fire,
> Impendent horrors, threat'ning hideous fall
> One day upon our heads.[3]

Copying out *Paradise Lost* word for word bears a certain relationship to stockpiling ammo. They're both rote, boring chores with no clear end in sight, only an ominous notion that what you're doing might be crucial to your private survival. There's also considerable vanity involved, much of it connected to a yearning for iconoclastic specialness, a preternatural and self-congratulatory awareness of what is and is not important in this world. Of course, copying out *Paradise Lost* isn't likely to lead to an all-night stakeout with a county deputy or a girlfriend drunkenly shot in the head. Nor is it a particularly effective tool for manipulating existential loneliness into manic paranoia. But the task has, more than anything else I've ever done, forced me to recognize that an artist risks damnation to create greatness . . . in Milton's case, *really* risks damnation. Satan is terrifying precisely because he's too human. He's a breathing, shouting, whispering, pain-filled, pride-filled, cocky, nervous, funny-looking, overconfident blowhard and lover of beauty. He stockpiles ammo, and he believes in conspiracy theories with all his heart. He's a Man so lovable and pitiable that any one of us might have shacked up with him in a cabin hidden off a black-dirt track; any one of us might have loved him, until the day he shot one of us in the head.

For me it was like a shot in the head to realize that Milton, a man who relied implicitly on the word of God, a man who repeatedly risked death for the sake of his religious and political beliefs, had laid his eternal soul on the gridiron to invent one of the rare literary characters who will survive in our tradition until the planet explodes, a character rich beyond any king in his confusion and high-strung self-importance; in his bony sensitivity and reluctant, persistent evil; in his neurotic, brilliant glare. And for so doing, Milton may indeed be weltering in the very hellfire he imagined, paying eternally for his hubris.

Which reduces my own vanity to a pocketful of beans. That happens often when I'm copying out *Paradise Lost*. Frequently a half-hour spent with the poem has an unpleasant yet bracing likeness to spilling cold water down my boot. Given the seriousness of the writer's undertaking, my comparison sounds flippant; but physical analogy can sometimes be the only handhold in the squirming struggle between myself and a prickly work of art. As Milton himself notes,

> Strength and Art are easily outdone
> By Spirits reprobate, and in an hour
> What in an age they with incessant toil
> And hands innumerable scarce perform.[4]

That tension is borne out by his own outrageous images, which, in the most solemn situations, roar in like clown cars. (His Eden boasts "Groves whose rich Trees wept odorous Gums," but all I can picture is a really bad place to park.) Yet the poem's descent into goofiness doesn't detract from its austerity. Accidents happen; even in paradise, you run the risk of getting gum in your hair; but the tale itself is inexorable.[5]

The half-accident of living in Harmony, the half-accident of copying out *Paradise Lost*—in both cases my initial desultory dalliance kept me ignorant of their physical power to absorb me. "Outsider status" is a tempting and often relevant conceit, a convenient label for loneliness, a watcher's cultural press pass. It's a tourist visa, a scholarly stamp of detachment, an artist's fishy eye. For me, however, it's become an increasingly fraudulent state of affairs, in part because it implies a meaningless superiority of intent (my ammo is better than your ammo), in part because I have come to find it impossible to maintain any clear DMZ between "out there" and "in here." It's like trying to parse the "Hee for God only, Shee for God in him" conundrum. If the marriage works, what difference does it make?

I can't think of anyone in Harmony who gives a damn about this kind of issue. Whether they're aging hippie factory workers or pregnant garbage-truck drivers pumping gas at Morrison's Garage, they've got better things to do than waste time decoding such niceties. Sure, all the Chadbournes live on the Chadbourne Road; all the Traftons live on the Trafton Road; and people from away will always be from away, even if they've lived here for fifty years. But on the whole, the citizens of Harmony don't much care. Nor do they much care about what peculiar hobbies you pursue in your winter-lit corner. Copying *Paradise Lost* may be a loony occupation, but so is spelling out your name in fir branches, decorating with Budweiser cans, building canoes without power tools, bottling pickled eggs, restoring antique tractors, and praying.

When you live in a town that sees snagging a job as a kindergarten teacher or a per diem nurse as proof you've clambered high up the economic ladder, concepts of work and accomplishment bear only a vague resemblance to the stampede for status that is routine in academic and professional spheres. No one in Harmony dreams of earning an endowed chair or a partnership. Success means talking your neighbor into letting you clear-cut forty acres of softwood. One can argue, justly, that a town like this has no future. But in a town without a future, the currencies of exchange are reduced to the present and the past; and a place's lingering vitality derives from how the townspeople hoard and spend that petty cash.

As Tom and I found out quickly, much of Harmony's petty cash is spent on inquiring into everyone else's business. Within days of our arrival, strangers started wandering up to us at the dump or the store, remarking, "I see you had company from New York," or "That bamboo you're weeding? It'll grow right back." It wasn't charming. It was scary. Years in the suburbs and the city had made me so used to public anonymity that flagrant personal interest felt like a threat. What was I doing wrong? What did they expect from me?

In other words, when I was confronted with plain childlike curiosity, my immediate response was panic. This seems terrible to me: that people are afraid that a guy driving by in a dump truck might notice what they're digging up in the yard, while at the same time they desperately pursue tenure and promotion without any suspicion those insignia might be pacifiers or shams. If nothing else, living in Harmony has taught me that nosiness is a unit of care.

But nosiness doesn't necessarily imply interference. When faced with wacky tendencies such as writing poems or spinning bunny fur, people don't ignore them so much as nod and shrug, as they might when lounging against a fence to watch a cattle show: bemused bystanders with nothing to say against prodding a cow to trot around a sawdust ring; they wouldn't prod a cow themselves, but they've heard of folks who like that sort of thing. They're attentive but not meddlesome. Nor do they rank watching a cattle show as more or less important than watching a sheep show or a swine show. It's an attitude implying that nothing much matters. But it also opens the possibility that anything might matter ... even everything.

> So from the root
> Springs lighter the green stalk, from thence the leaves
> More aery, last the bright consummate flow'r.[6]

Discovering that my fellow citizens cared about who I was but not especially about what I did was a great liberation. "Unconditional love" is too sentimental a reduction, for the knowledge didn't release me from culpability. Free will is a fine and dangerous gift, but

> God made thee perfect, not immutable;
> And good he made thee, but to persevere
> He left it in thy power, ordain'd thy will
> By nature free, not over-rul'd by Fate
> Inextricable, or strict necessity.[7]

I've had the free will to make plenty of stupid public errors since I've been here, and people haven't overlooked them. I've also made plenty of stupid secret ones. But that isn't the point: Eve's mistake is everyone's mistake; and as nitwits, we're all in the same boat. Nor do I claim that finding a home is like unbolting the front door to a happy ending. Anyone who's read Laura Ingalls Wilder's *Little House* books knows that settling down is just the beginning of hardship.

At some prior juncture of this ramble I speculated that, among other things, *Paradise Lost* was both Milton's private lament and a poem about making do. Unlike most of us, fretting our lives away over routine troubles, Milton was the kind of man who woke up in the middle of the night agonizing over humanity's inability to manage free will; and in his poem he worries and worries over it, sometimes bombastically, sometimes in lines that are touchingly bewildered. When Raphael explains the concept of free will to Adam, he reminds him it's a gift with a catch: "if ye be found obedient." Adam is immediately confused:

> But say,
> What meant that caution join'd, *if ye be found*
> *Obedient?* can we want obedience then
> To him, or possibly his love desert
> Who form'd us from the dust, and plac'd us here
> Full to the utmost measure of what bliss
> Human desires can seek or apprehend?[8]

What could be simpler than obedience? But when it means squelching the curiosity that makes us human—intellectual curiosity! Milton's own particular God-given pleasure!—the requirement is as impossible as informing a hound he's not allowed to smell. No wonder Adam is confused and Milton is grieving. Our fallen state is an indelible sorrow; for even with a second, a third, a fourth chance, we'd eat that apple all over again. People never learn. Just ask Pandora and Bluebeard's wife.

What we're left with is making do.

THIS MORNING, first light of a new year, I wake knowing that my car has a flat tire and we're almost out of dog food. Sleet rattles against the roof. Through the window daylight pulses and shivers like the wan, ticking breath of snow. I sigh and roll out of bed, clump downstairs, rake the dead ashes from the woodstove. I light a fire that sputters, but it stays lit: that's a small triumph.

At the kitchen sink I run hot water into a five-gallon water carrier; after months in an unheated barn, old goats need a hot drink to stay alive. I swath myself in coat, boots, gloves, scarf, hat. I collect a pail of scraps for the chickens, heave the water carrier out of the sink. I stump outside into the wretched morning, draped with burdens. I am not in a good mood.

Beyond the tree line, a town snowplow clanks and scrapes, far away, now closer, close, too close, a roar, and fading now, far away, groaning and muttering, a distant scratch, gone.

A crow shouts once and falls silent.

Now the only sound is sleet, clicking, whispering, pecking the plastic sled my sons have abandoned in the driveway, wriggling a grainy trail between my scarf and my neck. The crow shouts; another shouts back.

I park the water carrier in a snow crevice and work my gloved hand into the container's narrow handle, seeking a better grip, trying to save myself from getting wet. Eventually I start my trudge toward the barn. On alert, the goats begin bawling: hurry! hurry! The splayed spruce branches glitter ominously under their ice load. Happy New Year. Hunger and cold. Today's thin snow doesn't hide yesterday's frozen boot tracks.

"If ye be found obedient." How can I be otherwise? If I don't feed and water the animals, they'll die. My instructions are clear, my guilt poised and sensitive as antennae. But what about these circumstantial pleasures, these amusements and distractions that insist on surfacing, even as I bask in the grumpy glow of self-pity? Bragging crows and bossy goats, the fragile tick of sleet on the scrap pail, the cozy scrape of a snowplow taking care of business. That plow driver: this morning he's been obedient way longer than I have. His belly's bumping up against the steering wheel; he's draining the dregs of a giant paper cup of cold coffee and smoking his fifth cigarette as the defroster clears a vignette frame of windshield fog and slush. I send both of us good wishes for a long afternoon nap. In the meantime, we'll make our rounds.

> Meanwhile enjoy
> [Our] fill what happiness this happy state
> Can comprehend, incapable of more.[9]

3

Wild Invention

About them frisking play'd
All Beasts of th' Earth, since wild, and of all chase
In Wood or Wilderness, Forest or Den.

I HAD SOLVED THE MYSTERY of Milton's rhythmic line. Clots of verse throbbed down the page; what I read was a hidden music, not language. It was a vast discovery . . . I had found the template . . . quivering, exalted, I opened my eyes. My hot pillow had buckled into miserable lumps, the lines cascading away from me, sucked down into the drain of dreams. The clock ticked; my husband coughed once, coughed again, sighed, and burrowed his head into the comforter. I heard Mathilde the barn dog barking, barking, barking in the still night.

Later, scooping Purina into the dog's cracked rubber bowl, I thought with regret of the birds outside Virginia Woolf's window, the ones she heard when she was mad: the birds that sang in Greek.

I wasn't exactly wishing that the dog had been barking at owls in blank verse and stately metaphor. More, I was wishing I could delude myself into believing she had been. We can be jealous of madness, not for the misery of it but in admiration of a grand mind's grand errors. At one terrible crisis, Robert Lowell mistook himself for Milton. The hubris is breathtaking, unimaginable. What kind of twentieth-century man could possibly mistake himself for the exalted, the valiant, the vainglorious Milton—God's mouthpiece, Satan's confessor? My nearest approach is pretending to imagine that I heard my dog bark in Miltonic syllables: thickets, silence, showers of gold.

Imagination is a poet's lead rope, yanking us by the nose into collision with words, thoughts, sounds. It's also self-conscious, self-layered, and coy; we toy with our own cleverness, play-act a pretense of pretending. The spores of imagination grow from both what we don't know and what we take to be truth. But as our culture's scientific certainty hardens, we find it increasingly difficult to run riot in the fields of ignorance. Our imaginative scope retreats into crannies and cupboards, into the minutiae of the mind: what did I wear? who touched my hand? how salt were my tears? We no longer create gods.

Reading *Paradise Lost* is like tumbling off the dock into a green and foreign sea: the geography is physically precise, but the signs are strange. Traveling through the realms of Chaos, Satan asks "the Anarch old / with faltr'ing speech and visage incompos'd" for directions to earth; and in answer Chaos complains, like a cranky Natty Bumppo, about the sprawl of settlements encroaching on his territory:

> first Hell
> Your dungeon stretching far and wide beneath;
> Now lately Heaven and Earth, another World
> Hung o'er my Realm, link'd in a golden Chain

To that side Heav'n from whence your Legions fell:
If that way be your walk, you have not far.[1]

Briefly the map seems clear enough to follow. Beneath the barren waste of Chaos looms hell; above it, heaven has recently appeared and now, more lately, earth. But here the geography becomes confusing: if earth is "link'd in a golden Chain / To that side Heav'n from whence your Legions fell," is it still a place on the map? Or has it become a different sort of possession, more akin to a watch on a watchguard, a dog on a leash? Is heaven both an actual territory and an actual chain hook?

When I reach moments like these in the poem, I fretfully snap my computer shut and go downstairs, searching for something to do, maybe fold towels or water a houseplant, that doesn't tax my powers of invention. Naturally, I admire the quirks and coils of Milton's serpentine imagination—"Insinuating, wove with Gordian twine / His braided train." But I have to play back those images, track those torsions, devious and convolute, in my head as I read; and his bizarre descriptive leaps and corkscrews are exhausting. Trying to make sense of them can feel like playing pinochle with a deck of crawling insects.[2]

Why is it so hard for me to plot a route on Milton's arcane maps? Perhaps it's an atrophied sense of wonder, the cultural hardening I mentioned a few paragraphs ago, though now I wish I hadn't thought of it. Losing wonder: what a terrible notion. But truly, who in this century can imagine the earth as a golden bauble dangling from heaven's belt—not as a metaphor but as a solid sphere? Our preconceived factual images are too strong to displace. Even fantasy novels fit their conceits of time travel and aliens into contemporary conceptions of the universe, just as religious tracts left in the ladies' bathroom at the Skowhegan State Fair shrink the image of God to the scale of an extra-tough high school principal.

If I often find it difficult to imagine what Milton has invented, I find it equally difficult to imagine *how* he invented it. To me, writing a poem feels like laying bricks, in sun, in rain, week after week after week, all the while expecting that cold north wind, inspiration, to roar in and pelt me with rubble. As I mutter over this graceless task, I pick and choose among my materials—bits of language, music, form, memory, knowledge, fancy; and gradually these bits, planed or pebbled, mundane or rare, accrue into chunks of image and narrative that may smoothly adhere or abjectly crumble or box me up in a dungeon.

Presuming that Milton composed in some parallel fashion, I wonder how much of *Paradise Lost* was conceived by artisan intent, how much by accident: images bursting their bonds, shooting like random comets into the fifth dimension, while the poet lay back in his chair and listened for thuds and explosions. Sometimes when I start untangling the opening phrases of his outsized comparisons, I can almost feel his thoughts banging around inside his skull, like Athena inside Zeus's head, ready to erupt in full armor. Armed with what, though? I wonder if Milton had any notion of where those comparisons were traveling. Or was he just as surprised as I am at how they turned out? Take this description of Satan, weltering with the other fallen angels in their lake of hellfire:

> Thus Satan talking to his nearest Mate
> With Head up-lift above the wave, and Eyes
> That sparkling blaz'd, his other Parts besides
> Prone on the Flood, extending long and large
> Lay floating many a rood, in bulk as huge
> As whom the Fables name of monstrous size,
> *Titanian*, or *Earth-born*, that warr'd on Jove,
> *Briareos* or *Typhon*, whom the Den
> By ancient *Tarsus* held, or that Sea-beast
> *Leviathan*, which God of all his works

Created hugest that swim th' Ocean stream:
Him haply slumb'ring on the *Norway* foam
The Pilot of some small night-founder'd Skiff,
Deeming some Island, oft, as Seamen tell,
With fixed Anchor in his scaly rind
Moors by his side under the Lee, while Night
Invests the Sea, and wished Morn delays:
So stretcht out huge in length the Arch-fiend lay.[3]

It begins, vividly enough, describing the vastness of the Fiend and then marches portentously into a comparative litany of classical giants and monsters and the biblical sea serpent Leviathan. All this, while impressive, is not necessarily astonishing. I understand that Satan is enormous on an epic scale, as I understand that the Andromeda galaxy is enormous on an epic scale; but hearsay blunts and diminishes my perceptions. It's a case of pretending to imagine, though the pretense is agreeable, even comprehensible, in a motion-picture sort of way.

But behind this orotund fleet of giants flounders the brief, almost throwaway image of a hapless pilot "on the *Norway* foam" in "some small night-founder'd Skiff," who mistakes the "scaly rind" of the Leviathan for an island and unwittingly anchors his boat to the monster. His fate is clear; anyone can predict what's bound to happen next ... and at this terrible interstice, Milton pauses. It's like one of those nightmares when I know I should run but suddenly my legs are paralyzed. I wait for the Leviathan to swish his massive tail and consign the poor skiff to Davy Jones's locker. I wait and I wait, but nothing happens. "While Night / Invests the Sea, and wished Morn delays," I'm left staring at the page, the pilot's boat is left moored to the Leviathan, and the poet calmly sails away into the plot.

There's a cruelty to the image, a disregard, that's painful. It's not clear to me that the pilot matters to Milton; it's not clear to me that

Milton even intended to mention his plight. The image is so small, so intimate, compared to the vastness of its predecessors. The words are tacked onto the ornate litany with a quick, loose stitch, like a raw cotton panel basted to a margin of the Bayeux tapestry. As a semi-scholarly reader, I know I should make allowances for time and space: the preoccupations of a male Puritan intellectual in mid-seventeenth-century London cannot mirror the preoccupations of a belletrist housewife in early twenty-first-century Maine. But the fact remains that we lock horns with books on our own terrain. We argue with them as ourselves, not as ideal readers. Milton did not respond to the myths of Titanian and Typhon as an ancient Greek but as a modern radical Christian with bad eyes and wife trouble, making leaps and assumptions that would no doubt have bewildered Sophocles.

So I'm anxious about the pilot's skiff, and I'm annoyed with Milton for leaving him in the lurch, without even a decent funeral. Yet at the same time I sense that the episode's tacked-on quality indicates a shift—maybe even a lapse—in rhetorical and imaginative attention that, whatever it does for the poem, reconfigures my notions of the man. He assumes a vaguely Mr. Micawberish air. I picture him thrusting his hand into the bosom of his shabby shirt and coughing, "Ahem," before launching into his next logorrheic disquisition. As Samuel Johnson famously commented about *Paradise Lost*, "none ever wished it longer." Perhaps Milton wasn't always an alabaster bust. Maybe every once in a while he was a garrulous speechmaker prone to talk first and think later.[4]

While *Paradise Lost* is no *comédie humaine*, Milton himself lived in the thick of the real: sparrows and woolen stockings, chamber pots and horse manure. If I forget the poet was a real man, I do so because the poem purposely conceals his individuality beneath a storehouse of pompous language and moral polemic, as in tiresome passages like this one:

All who have thir reward on Earth, the fruits
Of painful Superstition and blind Zeal,
Naught seeking but the praise of men, here find
Fit retribution, empty as thir deeds.[5]

This is a far cry from the urge of most contemporary poets, who create purely from the personal, whose polemic is snide and shrill, arising from the flaws of congressmen, not angels. In such passages Milton's voice isn't pleasant or even recognizably human. Unlike Dante, he's not concerned with the breathing, shouting, groaning, laughing, wailing sea of human souls, past, present, or future. He's God's spokesman, and he's not interested in my feelings. Really, by copying out *Paradise Lost* word for word, the greatest leap I take as a belletrist housewife living in early twenty-first-century Maine may be the risk of discovering nothing about myself, either as "I" or as a citizen of history.

As it's turned out, my relationship with the poem is more complex than my preconceptions. Yet the further I wander, the more I realize that Milton himself was treading a new path in the epic by following the lead of his own curiosities, his own observations, his own rhetorical blind alleys. It's as if he meant to be Chapman's Homer but kept slipping up and being regular old Milton.

I don't mean to imply that *Paradise Lost* is a confessional poem masquerading as thundering rhetoric. For instance, it's tempting to believe that the pilot episode reveals a fraction of the poet's personal existential suffering; but I think, given how ruthlessly Milton maroons the boat, that's too Romantic a reading. Even if the scene is a lapse into the personal, it's a tiny stumble. It does, however, hint at why poets like Shelley and Keats pored over *Paradise Lost* as if it were a map to their own future. The poem is curiously prescient, in the oddest places.

Animals, for instance. To me, Milton's imaginative rendering of the animal-human connection is upsettingly familiar. I have long been aware that my relationships with animals are idealized, selfish, and ambiguous. As Milton points out, in the history of civilization, this is nothing new. Even the joys of prelapsarian farming don't hide the fraught nature of that bond.

Anyone who loves his dog can tell you that animals are, among other things, very entertaining. But why? They're just going about their business. They're not trying to be funny. For instance, when my hens hop out the door on a winter morning, they don't mean to slip on the ice. Yet sometimes they do: and really, there's nothing funnier than watching a chicken slip on the ice: her short legs fly straight out from under her; she lands flat on her tail feathers and sails squawking across the chicken yard like a fat kid at a sledding party.

Why is that scene so funny? Because the hen looks "like a fat kid at a sledding party." If she just looked like a hen, she wouldn't be funny at all. What's comic is the intersection between accidental chicken behavior and purposeful human behavior, and the stodgy term *anthropomorphism* doesn't quite capture the imaginative swiftness of the link. Our animals, at such slapstick moments, are prancing, leaping figures of speech.

But in Eden, the human-animal relationship is both more deliberate and more detached. After dinner Adam and Eve "recline / On the soft downy Bank damask't with flow'rs," ready to enjoy a friendly circus:

> Sporting the Lion ramp'd, and in his paw
> Dandl'd the Kid; Bears, Tigers, Ounces, Pards
> Gamboll'd before them, th' unwieldy Elephant
> To make them mirth us'd all his might, and wreath'd
> His Lithe Proboscis.[6]

"Hey, fellas! Let's put on a show for the nice people!" Is this what animals were like before the Fall?

If you feel that you've seen this picture before, you're right: you've seen it in storybooks, in toy stores, on cards and bibs and sweatshirts. The idealization of animals is endemic. Our culture seems to have a massive urge to invert the definition of wildness: let's imagine the perfect wild beast as a creature that tames itself just to make humans happy! Even Harmony, land of deer hunting and bear baiting, is typical as far as stuffed animals go. Tire salesmen court postal workers with teddy bears; large middle-aged cooks sport Tweety Bird overalls.

But who would have thought Milton, of all men, would be a sucker for *cute*?

True, Eden can't be paradise if lions are busy acting like lions—fierce, fast, and rapacious. Cute lions solve that problem: they're not only decorative but also static and safe; and Eden is perfect only as long as everything remains perfectly predictable: "the compliant boughs" yield supper; "sporting the lion ramp[s]"; Eve and Adam walk "hand in hand, . . . the loveliest pair / That ever since in love's imbraces met."[7]

Yet even in paradise, the human-animal bond has its complications. Consider this appalling pronouncement:

> Man hath his daily work of body or mind
> Appointed, which declares his Dignity,
> And the regard of Heav'n on all his ways;
> While other Animals unactive range,
> And of thir doings God takes no account.[8]

I hate this passage. It's painful, in the way it hurts to overhear someone say your child is ugly. Surely God loves what I love! No such luck, declares Milton without a shrug. And once again, he sails off into the plot, leaving the cute animals hopping and cavorting like wind-up toys.

Eden may be a human paradise, but for animals it's more like limbo—a garden of restraint, even oblivion, where showing off for humans is as close as a beast ever gets to God. Perhaps this accounts for the desperation of "th' unwieldy Elephant," who "to make them mirth us'd all his might." But "all his might" isn't good enough. Barring Milton's silly "wreath'd / His Lithe Proboscis," the sporting-and-gamboling episode is remarkably unfunny. It's club-footed and ponderous—nothing at all like watching a hen slip on the ice in my chicken yard.

What's missing in his scene is believable human-animal interaction, which is strange, considering that Milton has gone out of his way to paint Eden as Happy Animal Farm. In our fallen world, farmers and livestock interact. The nature of that interaction varies infinitely, but whether they share a backyard pig pen or a six-hundred-cow dairy, animals and people adjust and readjust their bonds. When Ezra the backyard pig glimpses a woman walking by the fence with a long stick, he ambles over in case she feels like scratching his back. When milk cow #45 sees a man with a bucket stride by at sundown, she bellows to remind him she likes grain. The people mostly respond obligingly. Both parties expect it. Otherwise, the animals would have initiated the episodes differently—maybe waddled away from the woman with the stick or kicked at the man with the bucket.

But for whatever reason, Milton's invention doesn't extend that far. He's pretending to imagine Happy Animal Farm, but the animals are fake and the keepers oblivious. Didn't an obstreperous cat ever arrange herself on his papers and obnoxiously wash herself? Thus far in my perambulations through *Paradise Lost*, the only time I'd guess it is when Satan gets involved.

> Down he alights among the sportful Herd
> Of those four-footed kinds, himself now one,
> Now other, as thir shape serv'd best his end
> Nearer to view his prey, and unespi'd

> To mark what of thir state he more might learn
> By word or action markt: about them round
> A Lion now he stalks with fiery glare,
> Then as a Tiger, who by chance hath spi'd
> In some Purlieu two gentle Fawns at play,
> Straight couches close, then rising changes oft
> His couchant watch, as one who chose his ground
> Whence rushing he might surest seize them both
> Gript in each paw.[9]

Clearly, Milton equates wild animal nature with evil; is there any other way to read this passage? But as poetry, it stalks and leaps and rushes. It reminds me of those other great cat poems—Blake's "The Tyger," Rilke's "The Panther": language drenched in *cat*. It's so much more vivid than "th' unwieldy Elephant" passage, which is just as clumsy as its subject.

But the thing that gets me is that Adam and Eve don't notice the difference. This tiger could be exactly the same tiger as the one who gambols so boringly with the bears, ounces, and pards. All Adam does is start a new conversation with Eve about how happy he is. All Eve does is "[turn] him all ear to hear new utterance flow." No matter what the animals do, the farmers remain preoccupied with themselves.[10]

This is the crux of my discomfort. I can put up with cute. I can put up with the tamed-beast analogy for paradise and its flip side, the wild beast as analogy for evil. I accept the various ramifications that arise in regard to my own interactions with the parakeets who chirp in my house and the chickens who squawk in my yard. I see my standing-in-the-shoes-of-God culpability for the life and death of these animals, whether I ask the vet to euthanize the dog who bit my son in the face or I raise a pig to be friendly primarily so he'll be easier to catch when slaughter time comes around. My relations with animals are morally ambiguous; and though I don't believe I'd resolve that ambiguity by foreswearing leather shoes and feeding Vegi-Cat to the housepets, I try to be candid about my responsibility and my guilt—candid to myself, to my sons, to my vegetarian parents; candid, as best I can, to the animals in my care.

And I do try to pay attention to the animals.

I've said that *Paradise Lost* is prescient in the oddest places; and sometimes a sort of divine omniscience seems to curl like smoke from the poem's various, strange, oxymoronic clashes. Milton's imagination is both extraordinarily mannered and extraordinarily supple. His persona can be cold and forbidding in one section and boyishly eager in another. On one level, I can't understand how Eve and Adam, our supposedly perfect ancestors, could have remained so ignorant of the panting, growling, scratching, rolling lives around them. On another level, I see that their attitude is indeed at the root of human perfection. We, who blithely assume "so many signs of power and rule," "who enjoy / Free leave so large," who waste hours sifting the treasure and dross of our own minds: we are their descendants.[11]

The animals, meanwhile, "unactive range, / And of thir doings God takes no account."

So I ask myself, "What are the goats doing in the barn while I'm sitting upstairs at my desk copying out *Paradise Lost*?" Milton already knew the answer. For the truth is: I have no idea. And I'm not running outside to find out.

4

The Undefiled Bed

Hail wedded Love, mysterious Law, true source
Of human offspring, sole propriety
In Paradise of all things common else.

Though by now we've been married for nearly sixteen years, more than once Tom and I have announced over a beer that we'd never do it again. As far as I can tell, neither one of us is hinting at divorce. And as far as I can tell, our declaration isn't one of those conversational ice chunks that occasionally float up from the marital iceberg: those double-edged couple-ish remarks like "She doesn't eat parsnips, so I don't cook parsnips" or "I've always left the decorating up to you" or "He's never enjoyed talking on the phone." We in fact have an easygoing friendship, don't argue about child raising, admire each other's artwork, and can stack hay without quarrelling. So on the surface, it's strange that we've come to this conclusion about what appears to be a flourishing partnership.

I think one source of our antipathy is *getting* married. This, in itself, is odd because I (and even Tom—though being the skinny, silent type, he winces at the prospect of all overwrought public gatherings) actually enjoy attending weddings. My cousin's marriage to a remarkably large-breasted girl was, for instance, a very entertaining celebration. At the reception, which took place in a firehouse in central New Jersey, my generally self-contained mother drank cheap wine and danced recklessly to "Love Shack." The bride's satin skirt ripped out at the waistband during "YMCA" and had to be safety-pinned with much fuss and flurry, while the bride was screeching at Tom, crouched in a corner with his camera, "Hey! Are you taking any good photos of this?" The Presbyterian groom's family was confused by the ziti and sauce ("Who eats macaroni at a wedding?"), which the bride's Italian family insisted was de rigueur ("Everybody eats macaroni at a wedding!").

A wedding is one of the few celebrations in which people of all ages dress up in fancy outfits, consume ridiculous food, pace solemnly up and down aisles, cry in public, sing comic songs, hold hands with their fathers, and do the limbo. What can be wrong with an occasion that jumbles together high ceremony and cheerful absurdity to celebrate a new bond? It seems, in some ways, an ideal amalgam of human social relations.

Yet when I'm chipping away at *Paradise Lost* and happen across lines like these, where Adam and Eve are getting ready for bed, I feel a twinge of regret:

> other Rites
> Observing none, but adoration pure
> Which God likes best, into thir inmost bower
> Handed they went; and eas'd the putting off
> These troublesome disguises which wee wear,
> Straight side by side were laid.[1]

For a poet so addicted to syntactic contortion and celestial for-
mality (especially in matters of battle: how he loves a stately clash),
Milton's thoughts about marriage are notably modest, even austere.
To begin with, he equates lapsarian marriage with clothes, and he
cannot stand "these troublesome disguises." He's so vehement, in
so many places, about how awful they are that I frivolously begin
to wonder if he had a wool allergy, or maybe a mole on the back
of his neck that chafed against his collar, or perhaps was married
to an inept seamstress. Trivializing is unfair, however, because his
diatribes against clothing are, beneath their bluster, some of the
most poignant passages in the poem. For to Milton, humanity in
its naked glory most nearly replicates the beauty of the angels:

> Two of far nobler shape erect and tall,
> Godlike erect, with native Honor clad
> In naked Majesty seem'd Lords of all,
> And worthy seem'd, for in thir looks Divine
> The image of thir glorious Maker shone,
> Truth, Wisdom, Sanctitude severe and pure.[2]

In our fallen world, this vision of humanity is not only patently
false but even embarrassing. The rare beautiful bodies among
us are more renowned for stupidity than for "Truth, Wisdom,
Sanctitude severe and pure." As for the rest of us aging grunts,
our flabby, bony, pasty shells seem evidence of both physical and
metaphorical ineptitude—a frail, imploding carapace, a monstrous
rhinoceros suit, a winding sheet.

Milton's vision of human beauty charms me, and makes me
sad, because unlike our present conceptions of beauty, which are
so often narcissistic and self-flagellating and victimized and mob-
controlled, his depends on a shared, equivalent gaze. "Straight side
by side were laid" may be the starkest description of a marriage
bed I've ever read, an image more akin to a double funeral than a

honeymoon suite. But its starkness is also simplicity, and innocence, and, perhaps most movingly, concentration. Look only at me, my love, and I will look only at you.

Marriage is indeed a concentration: both an unswerving attention to another human being and the distillation, day by day, year by year, of what matters in a shared life. Since a wedding is a sloppy froth of cousins, ribbons, parents, pomp, cake, bad photos, and mishap, it seems like a silly way to begin such an enterprise. But I don't have anything against silliness, though clearly Milton didn't care to picture our noble First Parents as gigglers. What I hate is the idea of being looked at by all those wedding guests.

A wedding is a story with lots of characters. A marriage is a story with two. No matter how tightly it intersects with other family divisions—children, parents, cousins, ancestors—marriage itself is a separate world, remote as an island. Scanning the crowd of couples at a local basketball game, I note strange alliances and ponder unanswerable questions: "What does she see in that jerk?" or "How does it feel to wake up every morning next to such an enormous woman?" But I'll never know. Even children, those greedy observers, never in all their lives understand the secret links and fissures in their parents' union.

"Straight side by side were laid." This is what it feels like, marriage, on fine days and on bad days. Lately I tried to have a conversation with Tom on this very subject, as we paused together in the kitchen. The kettle hissed on the woodstove, and he was holding a wet dishtowel. I had propped a basket of folded shirts against my hip. Our sons had shot off into their own orbits, sorting through Legos or listening to Lone Ranger episodes or folding paper airplanes. It was a regular winter evening, cold and dark, and we were pleased to be together, though not talking about it. And then I tried to talk about it and found there was nothing to say. "Of course weddings are nothing like being married," he said.

"But that's what I'm trying to write about," I explained.

"But weddings are nothing like being married," he said.

I went up to bed feeling confused and disappointed. Had I expected some clarification, some revelation? Was I trying to articulate something too obvious to mention? Or was I misunderstanding some larger, more vital conceit? And then, unexpectedly, Tom followed me to bed almost as soon as I'd gone up—Tom, who likes to haunt the house late and alone: and that was a surprise and a pleasure; for we rarely have a chance to lie awake together, feeling the night chill seep through the window at the foot of the bed, feeling our own warmth seep from one quiet body to the next. And though I still had no clarification, no revelation, what I did have was comfort, the dozy, inarticulate comfort of contiguity, which has nothing to do with passion or epiphany but is a good end to a regular day.

Being fond of both Tom and the conjugal ideal, I find it easy to shuffle among such sentimental snapshots and pretend they render an honest portrait of marriage. Milton wasn't such a fool. Consider the tale of Sin, the "Portress of Hell Gate," who is Satan's daughter, born Athena-like from his head, and also mother of his monstrous son, Death:

> I pleas'd, and with attractive graces won
> The most averse, thee chiefly, who full oft
> Thyself in me thy perfect image viewing
> Becam'st enamor'd, and such joy thou took'st
> With me in secret, that my womb conceiv'd
> A growing burden.[3]

I think Milton intends the amours of Sin and Satan to work as a lewd parody of Eve and Adam's "bed . . . undefil'd." But how different is the pure, absorbed, human gaze from Satan and Sin's "Thyself in me thy perfect image viewing"? As a lapsarian wife, I find the distinction difficult to untangle, though I do see one other significant difference: modest Eve has plenty of unencumbered recreational sex, and flirty Sin instantly gets pregnant, after which everything goes downhill for her.[4]

God intended Eve to be "our general Mother"; and in theory, Milton is all for babies: "Our Maker bids increase, who bids abstain / But our Destroyer, foe to God and Man?" But the poet is squeamish. After Sin gets knocked up, Satan instantly deserts her, and I suspect Milton doesn't necessarily fault him for side-stepping the mess.

> Pensive here I sat
> Alone, but long I sat not, till my womb
> Pregnant by thee, and now excessive grown
> Prodigious motion felt and rueful throes.
> At last this odious offspring whom thou seest
> Thine own begotten, breaking violent way
> Tore through my entrails, that with fear and pain
> Distorted, all my nether shape grew
> Transform'd: but he my inbred enemy
> Forth issu'd, brandishing his fatal Dart
> Made to destroy: I fled, and cri'd out *Death*.

Death proceeds to rape his mother and beget a pack of "yelling Monsters," and the original unity of two dissolves into pain and chaos and misery.[5]

Is this hell? Or is it family life?

I didn't fall in love with Tom because I thought he'd make an excellent father of sons. I fell in love with the way the backs of his knees looked as he walked away from me down a dormitory corridor, the way his hair stuck straight up from his forehead in the mornings, the way he never bossed me around or made me play softball, the way he entered into the private lives of housepets, the way he stared up at the sky.

So loading children into a love affair's two-person rowboat is indeed a kind of hell. The boat rocks dangerously; it runs up against rocks and is menaced by sea serpents. Though I treasure my sons (and got pregnant on purpose), it took me all the years of their babyhood to reconcile myself to their random, interrupting confusions, to their demands and distractions, to how they sucked away my inner life and my married life. Given his high respect for both the unity of two and the fruits of his own imagination, Milton must have found the proximity of a wailing two-year-old in the kitchen nearly unbearable—as indeed, indeed, it is. I have knelt on that kitchen floor myself, wailing alongside that child. With diapers to pin and tantrums to strangle, who has time or space to "Sleep on, / Blest pair"?[6]

If, in my marriage, I'm grateful for our wordless moments of delight, I'm equally irritated and put-upon and distracted, willing to injure and be injured, to bitch when Tom doesn't wipe the kitchen counters after he's been roofing all day, to fight jealousy and feed its fires, to lie in bed and hope he'll be the one who gets up to deal with an unhappy child or a barking dog. Every day, I'm dissatisfied with my lot—sick of sweeping up the mud our boots have dropped, sick of washing the sheets our bodies have crumpled, sick of nurturing the sons we prize.

One day I told Tom I was glad to be married to him, and he said, "If you hadn't married me, you would have married someone else." Can you blame me when I cringe at the thought of enduring another wedding? For yes, he's right. I wanted a husband, and I have one. Therefore, I love him. Such an admission doesn't do much for my credibility as a well-read woman with feminist proclivities. But how more ambiguous than politics is marriage, "mysterious Law," "shot forth [with] peculiar graces"—a strange land, a faraway town, a garden, a shelter, a bed.[7]

For all of Milton's talk about male dominance and female

subjection—how Adam's "fair large Front and Eye sublime declar'd / Absolute rule," how Eve's "wanton ringlets . . . impli'd / Subjection"—he knew he had to deal with the biblical facts of the story: Eve talked Adam into eating the apple. "Subjection" may be "impli'd" and "Absolute rule" "declar'd"; yet even in the most autocratic of marriages, the power balance tips and sways, and a covert gesture can topple a fortress. Blame the Fall on Satan if you like, but Adam was already predisposed to please his wife. How could paradise be otherwise? Their perfect marriage was its own undoing.[8]

> Here Love his golden shafts imploys, here lights
> His constant Lamp, and waves his purple wings,
> Reigns here and revels; not in the bought smile
> Of Harlots, loveless, joyless, unindear'd,
> Casual fruition, nor in Court Amours,
> Mixt Dance, and wanton Mask, or Midnight Ball,
> Or Serenate, which the starv'd Lover sings
> To his proud fair, best quitted with disdain.
> These lull'd by Nightingales imbracing slept,
> And on thir naked limbs the flow'ry roof
> Show'rd Roses, which the Morn repair'd.[9]

Even though I know better, when I read this passage I want to believe it can be true for Tom and me, despite our lapses and angers. I'll happily attend your next "Mixt Dance, and wanton Mask, or Midnight Ball," but more than anything I want to be "lull'd by Nightingales" in my own narrow bed, listening to the vague thump of Tom's stereo in the darkroom, hoping he'll remember to stoke the woodstove before he comes up and knowing that, when he does, he'll embrace me, even though I might be too sound asleep to notice.

To me, the saddest word in the passage is "unindear'd." The tragedy it implies cuts me to the heart. For it's endearment, not romance or passion (lovely as both can be), that makes marriage a solace. On a late winter afternoon I sit on the school bleachers with my fidgety son Paul, watching the Harmony boys win their first basketball game of the season, waiting for the fourth period, when the coach will finally let my crabby, benchwarming son James snag two minutes of play. If Tom gets home from work soon enough, if he has time to change his filthy clothes and wash the sheetrock dust out of his sticking-up hair, he'll drop in; and sure enough, there he is now in the doorway—at forty, still thin and wary as a boy—paying his one dollar, pausing to let the players rush to the other side of the court; and now he's walking along the edge of the floor, scanning the bleachers, looking for me; and when he catches my eye, he hurries his step; he has a goal, an intention; he scoots up quickly to get out of the players' path and sits down behind me; I lean back into his knee, and he says, settling his knee against my spine, "You shoveled out my truck."

And I say, "I did."

And he says, "They're winning."

And I say, "They are."

"Perpetual Fountain of Domestic sweets." Why waste all that money on a wedding when this is what you get?[10]

5
Gardening

His praise ye Winds, that from four Quarters blow,
Breathe soft or loud; and wave your tops, ye Pines,
With every Plant, in sign of Worship wave.

Harmony is an unpropitious place to plant a garden. Jutting from the U.S. map like a gloomy granite outcrop, the northern half of Maine looks and feels more like New Brunswick than Massachusetts. Here in Somerset County, the growing season is ridiculously short: June, July, and August are the only reliably frost-free months. But even high summer isn't worry-free. Local history (via my friend Linda, whose family has lived on the Trafton Road for a hundred years or so) offers up numerous anecdotes of midsummer snow, not to mention ice-, rain-, and mud-sodden tales involving town fields, roads, ponds, snowmobiles, woodlots, barns, horses, and bulldozers. After a lifetime here, Linda is both a bad-weather specialist and living proof of how a determined girl can triumph over adversity. When the Trafton Road disappeared into a bog (sometime in the 1950s, I think), she walked more than a mile through the swampy woods, twice a day, to catch the schoolbus. And her plaid skirt *was still clean.*

Harmony thrives on winter. After Christmas, when the snow thickens and the thermometer plunges, local spirits become buoyant. Wind-chill camaraderie erupts among post office patrons, blowing and stamping in the mailroom like purple-faced kids trooping in from recess. At the garage I find myself sucked into the cheerful team sport of ridiculing the bus driver, who's embarrassed himself by canceling school for a storm that ended up dropping only six inches of snow: "The goddamn sun was shining at dinnertime!" Ice fishermen stock up on smelts and coffee brandy; and in my Monday poetry class, fourth graders pen enthusiastic odes to plow trucks and the winter sand pile.

The other seasons just can't compete. Even at its height, spring glances back beseechingly at winter. Gravel roads thaw into swamps, refreeze to gaps and ruts, collapse into streams and culverts. Paved roads buckle and split. Overnight, blacktop chasms heave into asphalt peaks sharp enough to shear off mufflers and tailpipes. Green narcissus tips thrust bravely into a chill wind, then yellow under a sudden fall of sleet. Turning over soil, my spade clanks against masses of frozen dirt, black and crystalline, like chunks of arctic coffee grounds.

Likewise, autumn is a last chance to grit your teeth for winter: bank the house foundation with mulch hay and pine boughs, split firewood and nag your kids into stacking it, shoot a deer and bleed out a pig, pick all the green tomatoes and hope at least a few redden in the house. Some years frost comes so early that I don't get a single vine-ripened tomato.

But summer, that intoxication; brief, fly-ridden hour: what a surreal span it is.

> Ye Mists and Exhalations that now rise
> From Hill or steaming Lake, dusky or grey,
> Till the Sun paint your fleecy skirts with Gold,
> In honor to the World's great Author rise,
> Whether to deck with Clouds th' uncolor'd sky,
> Or wet the thirsty Earth with falling showers,
> Rising or falling still advance his praise.[1]

In Harmony, in the summertime, frigid ponds lap against their mucky shores. Nights are suspiciously cool. Scrub poplar overtakes the stony fields. A general hysteria pervades. Work, work! Fun, fun! Hurry, hurry! If summer life in a Twain or an O'Connor tale has a lethargy, a somnolence, even in the midst of hard labor, here in Maine the season feels like a mistake. Plant! Mow! Weed! Pick!

There's none of this anxious haste about yard work in paradise. As Adam reminds his wife, gardening in Eden is pure pleasure, just as much fun as cuddling in leafy bowers and reclining among the gamboling lions.

> Tomorrow ere fresh Morning streak the East
> With first approach of light, we must be ris'n,
> And at our pleasant labor, to reform
> Yon flow'ry Arbors, yonder Alleys green.

He does point out that perfect weather and perfect soil create their own problems: even in Eden a gardener has his burdens.

> Our walk at noon, with branches overgrown,
> That mock our scant manuring, and require
> More hands than ours to lop thir wanton growth:
> Those Blossoms also, and those dropping Gums,
> That lie bestrown unsightly and unsmooth,
> Ask riddance, if we mean to tread with ease.[2]

But despite "those dropping Gums," gardening in paradise seems more akin to a pleasant stroll with your sweetheart (naked, sans

mosquitoes or sunburn) than to my grubby, sweaty skirmishes
with potato beetles and spruce roots.

When I was twenty-two, I worked for a year managing a dairy
operation in Vermont. In midsummer, an apprentice arrived—a
gangly, slow-talking young man from Galveston, Texas, with plans
to enter a Catholic monastery. First, though, he thought he'd spend
a little time "shepherding." It was soon evident that "shepherding"
meant reclining under a shade tree, watching cows and goats switch
their tails and peacefully crop grass. Maybe he saw himself, every
once in a while, gently picking up a fluffy, friendly kid and restoring it to its placid dam. Needless to say, things didn't work out
as planned. Seventeen-hour workdays, baling in thunderstorms,
lascivious goat sex, drunken farmhands, calf diarrhea, peanut butter and coffee sludge for every meal; and the final straw: when the
border collie stole his brand-new very large sneakers and buried
them in the manure pile, along with her collection of chicken feet.
He didn't last two weeks.

Every time I read Milton's pretty gardening passages, I suspect
the poet of similar fantasies. He was city-bred, after all, and a blind
bookworm besides; although as a citizen of a less convenient era,
he certainly had upfront knowledge of wastes and "wanton growth"
that the civilized urban intellectual may now choose to forget. Yet
he apparently felt no compunction about idolizing country life. Of
course, there's a long, long history of overblown pastoral poems, and
Milton, despite his cranky morals, rose to power in the heyday of
"shepherding." You can't blame all that stuff on Herrick, Lovelace,
and crew: Milton's own *Comus* is chock-full of "wood nymphs deck'd
with daisies trim" and "flowery caves" and "love-lorn nightingales"
and such. After force-feeding on *Paradise Lost*, I feel a bit queasy
browsing among the "pert fairies" and "dapper elves" of *Comus*. But
despite their aesthetic and narrative differences, the meditations on

landscape in both the masque and the epic are remarkably similar.
As the shepherd-sorcerer Comus remarks,

> Wherefore did Nature pour her bounties forth,
> With such a full and unwithdrawing hand,
> Covering the earth with odours, fruits and flocks,
> Thronging the seas with spawn innumerable,
> But all to please and sate the curious taste?[3]

Such a passage might have fallen straight out of *Paradise Lost*. No
matter how much Milton advanced as a thinker and an artist, he
never got to the point of conceiving that nature might be valuable
in and of itself. Nature is beautiful and desirable only insofar as it
makes its human residents happy and comfortable. Otherwise, a
garden is a wilderness and therefore dangerous if not downright
evil. You won't catch Milton squatting in muddy clay by a roaring
river, cutting fiddlehead ferns for dinner as blackflies swarm in
his hair and gnaw the backs of his ears. So what if a thrush sings
plaintively in a glade, a pair of wood ducks glides in, low and quiet,
over a snow-fed rill? If experiencing nature means sitting in mud
being devoured by insects, he'd rather miss it.

Milton's obstinate shepherding attitudes are at striking odds with
his austere vision of the marriage bond. When a poet so carefully
denotes the perfect marriage as a civil working partnership—"To
prune these growing Plants, and tend these Flow'rs, / Which were
it toilsome, yet with thee were sweet"—and exhorts that "Man
hath his daily work of body or mind," it does seem rather comic
that "daily work" involves nothing more strenuous than ambling
hand in hand down a path and twining a vine or two around a tree
before lunch. It's more like advertising copy for Chem-Lawn than
an actual description of "daily work"; and when I read it, I have the
alarming thought that Milton's image of Eden might be one root

cause of humankind's imbecile dealings with the environment. We may be fallen creatures, but we still expect nature to do our bidding: to suck in our coal smoke and auto exhaust with a whistle and a grin, yet pour forth her lovely, non-biting, non-poisonous gifts "profuse on Hill and Dale and Plain."[4]

Granted, I'm writing these thoughts in Maine in January, when the whole idea of wandering through a garden twining vines around trees seems mythic and overblown. The only path I can walk down is one I've dug out for myself with a shovel. A stroll across the yard requires donning several layers of clothing, giant insulated boots, and snowshoes and then tumbling into a drift every few steps as I break a trail through ten inches of snow. While this is more fun than it sounds, it would make a fairly crappy pastoral ode. For in the tradition of pastoral paeans, a human body is always fresh, comfortable, and natural in her environment, a scenario that is never possible in winter, unless the setting includes a swept hearth and a roaring fire.

So I'm torn when I read Milton's descriptions of Eden. His willful ignorance of the intricate relations between humans and the natural world irritates and sometimes horrifies me. But his false countryside also delights me, that "fringed Bank with Myrtle crown'd," "the crisped Brooks, / Rolling on Orient Pearl and sands of Gold." Though I have to ignore almost everything I actually know about real labor, when I read Milton's imagined paradise I can almost—almost—believe in a garden rich and lush enough "to give us only good." No blackflies here. Even among the prideful scrabblers of the earth, those of us who've spent the better part of an afternoon struggling to heave what looks like an asteroid out of a muddy cabbage patch or eradicate a grove of dandelions with foot-long taproots, there's seduction in the indolence of Eden.

> Under a tuft of shade that on a green
> Stood whispering soft, by a fresh Fountain side

They sat them down, and after no more toil
Of thir sweet Gard'ning labor than suffic'd
To recommend cool *Zephyr*, and made ease
More easy, wholesome thirst and appetite
More grateful.[5]

In midwinter, its seductions are far more alluring than they ever are in summer, when I'm spreading mulch and crushing slugs and clogging the mower blades with wet grass. Back in Vermont, besieged by thunderstorms and calf diarrhea, I didn't rustle up much pity for the future monk from Galveston. I admit I laughed when the dog buried his sneakers in shit. Yet these days I recall him more tenderly. If he wasn't very bright, he was exceedingly hopeful. After a lifetime's acquaintance with the blunt actualities of livestock, I'm not enticed by the romance of shepherding; but I have my rural fantasies.

Betwixt them Lawns, or level Downs, and Flocks
Grazing the tender herb, were interpos'd,
Or palmy hillock, or the flow'ry lap
Of some irriguous Valley spread her store,
Flow'rs of all hue, and without Thorn the Rose.[6]

Arcadia. It's the name of a broccoli variety I've been reading about in the Fedco seed catalog, a local supplier specializing in hardy varieties for non-Edenic gardens. Apparently, Arcadia "rocks in conditions that reduce other broccoli to compost," is extremely beautiful ("frosty bluish-green heads with very refined small beads"), yet is "big and rugged, standing up not just to heat, but also to rot, mildew and cold stress." So many allurements! How can I go wrong? I circle the order number in the catalog and turn my attention to the tomato section. Here's a variety, Rose de Berne, with copy that opens with a quotation from a Vermont grower: "Felt like I was a real farmer with these beauties!" This tomato is "no slouch in the appearance department either," being "unblemished" and "perfectly round," with "a rich sweetness the others can't match." I circle the order number and browse on.[7]

"To the heart inspires / Vernal delight and joy." Why do I keep hoping for tomatoes? I should just admit defeat and save the space for leeks, which I can still dig up in December. And tomatoes aren't the only thorn in my glove. Every year I have a disaster, often in the most unexpected places. Take broccoli, for example, that tough standby of northern gardens. Last summer, those "frosty bluish-green heads" were so infested with wriggling cabbage worms that my son Paul (usually indifferent to insects) ran screaming at the sight. When I say "thousands," I do not exaggerate. The chickens ate that crop.[8]

Gardening in Harmony is a challenge even for an expert grower, and I am about as expert a gardener as I am a fire-starter: I can get the job done, sometimes, but the results aren't always pretty. I have no scientific bent toward soil research or climate analysis, and I'm not very good at picturing end results: my April vision of a harmonious flowerbed is likely to be a tangled, sagging mass of undergrowth in August. After a dozen summers' worth of mistakes, I've conquered some basic problems. I can now grow excellent lettuce and beets. But I will never be able to learn how "the mantling Vine / Lays forth her purple Grape." Yes, it "gently creeps / Luxuriant" all over my herb bed, but its handful of grapes (if they bother to form at all) are as sour as rhubarb.[9]

Fortunately, unlike Adam and Eve, I don't also contend with a "sportful Herd" in my garden, at least not on daily basis. True, the deer gobble my kale every fall, raccoons decimate the corn, and one overexcited poodle can destroy an entire bed of spinach in thirty seconds. But other than insects (who are, I admit, fairly "sportful"), my garden's animal kingdom is represented primarily by toads and snakes, fine and charming ornaments who also eat mosquitoes by the pound.

> close the Serpent sly
> Insinuating, wove with Gordian twine
> His braided train, and of his fatal guile
> Gave proof unheeded.[10]

One of the few really great reasons to garden in Maine is the fact that we have no poisonous snakes. So I can greet every snake I see with pleasure, and I see many. In spring, still half-frozen from their winter's hibernation, they coil, transfixed, on the rocks and paths, quick tongues fluttering, quick eyes darting. Frequently I scoop them up with a shovel and relocate them to some less obvious patch of sun (the poodle is fond of killing snakes), but they pay no attention. The indifference of a cold snake is noteworthy.

Toads keep to themselves for longer, delaying their public appearance until mowing season, skipping clumsily away from the blades, eyeing me blandly from damp corners. (The poodle tried eating a toad once but didn't enjoy the flavor.) There's something joyful in the sight of a toad, joyful like the sight of my apple-bellied Uncle Melvin in hiked-up beige dress pants, smacking a canoe with a cane. I love to think of toads, pouchy and calm in their damp corners, ruminating over spiders and flies; I love to think of snakes, jewel-eyed, sunlight fingering their spines.

Ironically, however, these two garden helpmeets are the very animals that Satan chooses to mask his evil ingenuity, assuming their forms at opportune moments—for instance:

> Squat like a Toad, close at the ear of *Eve*;
> Assaying by his Devilish art to reach
> The Organs of her Fancy, and with them forge
> Illusions as he list, Phantasms and Dreams.[11]

This is a strange inversion of paradise: gardens may have lapsed into riot and disarray and labor become tedious and crude. Yet the snake and the toad, thriving in their old familiar bodies—

"insinuating" or "squat"—have become respectable human allies, even harbingers of hope.

I wonder if Milton noticed this strange shift in allegiance. It may well be that his blindness kept him from considering the issue. Maybe his easy-care paradise was to some degree a product of his isolation, his physical helplessness in the roughshod world. Without the accidental sight of a toad resting in the shady lee of a stable yard, of a tiny snake slipping into the crevice below a blue-grey cairn, he had only his inner eye to stimulate their image. To transform these silent creatures into Satan's tools, he had to assign them voices. The gift of tongues rendered them evil. Thus, as mute watchers in our lapsarian gardens, perhaps they regain a portion of their innocence.

Milton tells us that "God takes no account" of the doings of animals. It's a tragic statement yet freeing also. It leaves animals to their own devices. Adam and Eve ate the apple and corrupted humanity, but the purity of fauna and flora persists despite humanity's failure. Perhaps they manage as overlooked children manage, as the unremarked second son survives intact while the favored firstborn shatters. Weeds sprout from cracked asphalt. Flies buzz and bump against a winter windowpane. Adam, that teacher's pet, got plenty of attention; but what good did it do him in the end?[12]

Snow-covered, my garden plot snores and groans in its long sleep, nestled among worm casings and weed seeds and beetle larvae and chunks of ice. This might be the spring I'll finally grow asparagus worth cutting, grass-green and armored, supple as willow wands. This might be the spring I dig up the beds in disgust and toss the roots to the chickens.

"As Nature wills," of course, but I'm hoping for the best.[13]

6

Angels, Obedience, and ATVs

I might relate of thousands, and thir names
Eternize here on Earth; but those elect
Angels contented with thir fame in Heav'n
Seek not the praise of men.

ANGELS, as "eternize[d] here on Earth," tend to be a rather feminized and delicate lot, inclined, when adults, to wear limp ecru nightgowns and stare off dreamily into the distance; when children, to display much chubby thigh and damask cheek. This is not the case with the angels of *Paradise Lost*, though they are unquestionably handsome in classic Hermes-and-Apollo style. Take Raphael, for instance, with his gorgeous and sultry wings:

> A Seraph wing'd; six wings he wore, to shade
> His lineaments Divine; the pair that clad
> Each shoulder broad, came mantling o'er his breast
> With regal Ornament; the middle pair
> Girt like a Starry Zone his waist, and round

> Skirted his loins and thighs with downy Gold
> And colors dipt in Heav'n; the third his feet
> Shadow'd from either heel with feather'd mail
> Sky-tinctur'd grain. Like *Maia's* son he stood,
> And shook his Plumes, that Heav'nly fragrance fill'd
> The circuit wide.[1]

But Milton's angels are more than gloriously attractive and good-smelling. Like the Greek gods and heroes, they're also tough. Heaven bristles with "thick embattl'd Squadrons bright, / Chariots and flaming Arms, and fiery Steeds / Reflecting blaze on blaze." Being "wont to meet / So oft in Festivals of joy and love," these angels aren't single-minded warriors like Ares or Achilles. They'd just as soon spend their time "Hymning th' Eternal Father." But when God talks, they listen:

> Go *Michael* of Celestial Armies Prince,
> And thou in Military prowess next,
> *Gabriel*, lead forth my armed Saints
> By Thousands and by Millions rang'd for fight;
> Equal in number to that Godless crew
> Rebellious, them with Fire and hostile Arms
> Fearless assault, and to the brow of Heav'n
> Pursuing drive them out from God and bliss.[2]

In Rome, an enormous bronze statue of the archangel Michael stands on top of the Castel Sant'Angelo, originally Hadrian's tomb, later a papal fortress and prison, with a wide stone ramp spiraling down the center, convenient for pouring forth soldiers, steeds, catapults, etcetera. When my friend Jilline and I first stepped into the building, she opened her arms and announced, "This would be a fabulous place to drive an ATV!" As soon as she spoke, our ears filled with the imagined echo of four-wheelers roaring up and down the dim passages of the Castel Sant'Angelo. We spent the rest of our visit expecting to be run over at any moment.

After my trip to Rome, every time I thought of the archangel Michael, I conflated my memory of the bronze's bright wings spreading into a cloudless sky with rampant ATV riding in a dark hallway. Though not yet Miltonic, my portrait of angels had already developed certain engine-revving, road-destroying characteristics at odds with the more prevalent Hallmarkian visions current in stores and churches. But ATVs are blocky and loud, mostly decorated with camouflage or rust, and distinctly earthbound; so I've spent some time trying to figure out why I keep picturing the archangel Michael driving one. It's not manliness; I do know that. Manliness has nothing to do with Milton's angels, who are far too pretty and intellectual. (Among angels, reason, by way of "Fancy and understanding," nourishes the soul—not a modern manly construct.) And at least in Harmony, manliness doesn't have much to do with ATVs. By the age of nine or so, most local boys have torn up numbers of fields and snowmobile trails on their four-wheelers. Parents tend to think of ATVs as starter cars for their kids, a good opportunity to practice sharp turns at high speed on rough terrain. This isn't to say that four-wheelers are strictly juvenile transportation. Hunters use them to haul heavy game out of the woods. A local woman drives hers out to the field twice a day when she fetches the cows for milking. A few seasons ago a teacher's aide took to commuting to school on his. Last year, during the Harmony Fair, an unidentified driver backed one into the rear passenger door of my car—at least that was the forensic conclusion of several very interested bystanders, who enjoyed examining the puncture marks and woefully shaking their heads. But despite their all-around usefulness in field and forest, ATVs retain an aura of youth, possibly because they have limitations (small size, no roof or truck bed, plus they're not street legal) that cut significantly into a driver's independence.[3]

In other words, while engines and guns are telltale signs of manliness in Harmony, even more they're signs of adult self-sufficiency: with a rifle and a Ford, you have the requisite tools for freedom. You can drive to the mall. You can put dinner on the table. Perhaps it's this issue of freedom, or lack of it, that allows me to envision Michael, Gabriel, and pals careening across a gravel streambed on their four-wheelers. They don't drive to the mall without asking their pa, and they never put dinner on the table. Like good boys, they show up promptly at mealtimes, where "Tables are set, and on a sudden pil'd / With Angels' Food" by "th' all bounteous King, who show'r'd / With copious hand, rejoicing in thir joy." Now, on nights when I'm roasting a chicken and my sons rush into the kitchen shouting, "What's for dinner? I'm starving! It smells great!" I feel just like God.[4]

It's not that I dislike Milton's angels. When the topic is glamour, I'm as impressed as Adam and Eve were:

> Haste hither *Eve*, and worth thy sight behold
> Eastward among those Trees, what glorious shape
> Comes this way moving; seems another Morn
> Ris'n on mid-noon.

Like Eve, I'd be running out of the house, dishcloth flying, to catch a glimpse of the archangel Raphael striding across my lawn. Like Adam, I would sit openmouthed over lunch as my guest explained that angels also

> contain
> Within them every lower faculty
> Of sense, whereby they hear, see, smell, touch, taste,
> Tasting concoct, digest, assimilate,
> And corporeal to incorporeal turn.
> For know, whatever was created, needs
> To be sustain'd and fed.[5]

What I can't abide is their obedience, and this disturbs me because it reveals both my flawed absorption of the poem as literature and my flawed apprehension of Milton's vision of humility.

One of the prickliest things to swallow in *Paradise Lost* is Milton's perpetual celebration of childlike good behavior, whether in warrior angels or modest wives or prancing tigers. "For this was all thy care / To stand approv'd in sight of God." No wonder Satan is so appealing. He's the only character with gumption enough to take charge of his own destiny. He's not noble and he's not right, but he's recognizably himself, which is more than I can say for the faithful angels. I can't tell one Good Citizen from the next, and I'm always getting their speeches mixed up and their names confused. Uriel, Abdiel . . . why even bother giving them names when their actions are so identically excellent?

> Thee Father first they sung Omnipotent,
> Immutable, Immortal, Infinite,
> Eternal King; thee Author of all being.[6]

If I can picture Raphael's six feathered wings and "downy Gold" thighs, why can't I willingly suspend my earthly notions of blind obedience, despite its connotations of fascism and mob rule, and imagine it as Milton intends it to be understood: as a greater, starker service to truth and right? A reader shouldn't have to subscribe to a belief in order to accept it sympathetically within the borders of the work. For instance, when I read about Dinah Morris, the Wesleyan preacher in George Eliot's *Adam Bede*, I can easily acknowledge the truth of her obedience, even early in the novel, before Eliot fleshes out her character, when all I have to go on is a physical description far less beautiful than Raphael's:

> She held no book in her ungloved hands, but let them hang down lightly crossed before her, as she stood and turned her grey eyes on

the people. There was no keenness in the eyes; they seemed rather to be shedding love than making observations; they had the liquid look which tells that the mind is full of what it has to give out, rather than impressed by external objects. She stood with her left hand toward the descending sun; and leafy boughs screened her from its rays; but in this sober light the delicate colouring of her face seemed to gather a calm vividness, like flowers at evening.[7]

But when I read *Paradise Lost*, I can't summon up any sentiment that corresponds to the sympathy I feel for Dinah's earnest evangelism. Instead, I feel recalcitrant and sulky—not far different from how I felt when I was six years old, visiting my father's parents in New Jersey and enduring a saccharine farewell from the Reverend Schulte, who bugged out his eyes, patted me on the head, and assured me that God loved me. I refrained from snarling, "He does not!" but only because of the looming wrath of Grandmom. In a way, she was my stand-in for Milton's "Author of all being." No matter what I actually did or did not do before her eyes, my guilt in the matter was permanent, my obedience exacted without question.

There's a church in Parkman, Maine, that I often pass when I'm driving my sons north to piano lessons or Farm League games or the orthodontist. This church, which advertises itself as a "non-denominational, Bible-believing congregation for juniors and adults," is pretty and white and has a large lighted sign that spells out various inspiring messages aimed at needy passersby. Lately the sign's been hawking an especially great reason to attend Sunday services: once I'm saved, I'll no longer have to depend on myself.

Herein lies another source of my discomfort with Milton's obedient angels. A reader may insist that she shouldn't have to subscribe to a belief in order to accept it sympathetically within the borders of a work of literature. But an author is perfectly free to ignore that claim. George Eliot wrote movingly of Methodists even though she had publicly, and painfully, renounced her family's nonconformist

beliefs. This alone makes her depiction of evangelism more palat-
able to a doubtful reader such as myself. I feel comfortable with
her religious perplexities as well as her respect for faith. We loiter
together on that village green, bemusedly watching Dinah prepare
to preach the word of God. We care, we admire, but we'll return
to our secular pursuits when the moment is over.

Milton, on the other hand, wouldn't be caught dead loitering
on a village green with me. He's not interested in my palaver about
respect and doubt, nor does he care to create a collegial pact with
his readers, as Eliot does. Far from it. Like the message on the Parkman church sign, *Paradise Lost* refutes the importance of individual
volition: don't bother to think you can depend on yourself. But
Milton's view differs significantly from the blandishments of the
Parkman church, which coax me into believing I have a chance at
salvation if I act now, if I start going to church, if I give up my evil
self-governance and enter the fold. Wrong, says Milton. There's a
right way and a wrong way, and I've already blown it. As Abdiel
declares to Satan,

> No more be troubl'd how to quit the yoke
> Of God's *Messiah*: those indulgent Laws
> Will not now be voutsaf'd, other Decrees
> Against thee are gone forth without recall;
> That Golden Sceptre which thou didst reject
> Is now an Iron Rod to bruise and break
> Thy disobedience.[8]

I've tried to overcome my revulsion. I've tried to read Milton's
angels as characters; as literary tropes; as a host of spirits, handsome, strong, and well behaved. I've tried to follow the logic of
free will. Yes, Raphael declares that God allows his angels to
make their own decisions about loyalty: "Our voluntary service
he requires, / Not our necessitated." But if they don't "choose" to

serve, they're doomed. So I can't stop envisioning them as an immense band of Hitler youth—blond, good-looking, and blindly, dreadfully, helplessly obedient. It's nearly impossible to extend the childlike humility I felt under the wrathful eyes of my grandmother to the vast self-effacing humility of Milton's angels. My reaction, then, is a hideous mutation of Milton's intentions, for his image of heaven has distorted into my image of hell. And because of this perversion, vast stretches of *Paradise Lost* are lost to me. The chasm between author and reader becomes impossible to bridge, mutual sympathy negated; and I'm left standing on the brink with nothing but a basket of angelic artifacts to sift through—chariots, standards, swords, wings—distantly, dispassionately, as though I'm cross-examining sand.[9]

It's hard to gauge what humanity has lost when a reader can no longer absorb a work of literature in the way in which an author intended. Loss, of course, is endemic to literature because it is endemic to language. Yet we adjust to such losses, partly because we're so used to linguistic erosions, even in the small span of our own lives. Consider the volatility of slang, for instance: the task of explaining "old" slang such as *grody* and *valley girl* to my incredulous sons is fine preparation for a curious voyage through the mysteries of Chaucer's English. But misapprehension of a great work's central moral code is an indefinable yet enormous loss. Not only does it divorce the reader from true, intense participation in the work. It also means that, in the author's final reckoning, the work is a failure. How could Milton possibly be content to know that *Paradise Lost* has been stamped forevermore as a Great Book yet has not achieved its prime intent: to "justify the ways of God to men"?[10]

On the surface, *Paradise Lost* might have been composed by the least humble of men: no poem is stagier or more ornate, no poet bossier and more self-righteous. Yet its central instruction—do what God says, and don't ask questions—relies on a conception of deference, of utter submission, that is foreign to nearly all readers, no matter what religious beliefs we embrace or spurn. Even when we long for heavenly instruction and protection, for Gabriel's "strict watch that to this happy place / No evil thing approach or enter in," we also desire infinite latitude for error and forgiveness. We want to stand inside the story and outside it as well. We want to be ourselves without responsibility for being ourselves, and in such case *Paradise Lost* offers us no comfort.[11]

Standing on a cart on the village green, in her shabby black dress and plain cap, Dinah Morris says to her gaggle of listeners, "Why, you and me, dear friends, are poor. We have been brought up in poor cottages, and have been reared on oat-cake and lived coarse; and we haven't been to school much, nor read books, and we don't know much about anything but what happened just round us. We are just the sort of people that want good news."[12] How easy it is to love Dinah. And how ironic it is that Eliot's deft characterization and sympathetic portrayal of unlettered life and innocent belief live on in modern conservative Protestantism as Milton's far more rigorous vision does not.

For despite her author's own religious doubts, Dinah's preaching style is precisely reflected in the evangelism of rural Maine and elsewhere around this country. She embodies an anti-intellectual, folksy goodness that has almost nothing to do with her creator but everything to do with her creator's clear and tender vision of human weakness. We want to be saved from eternal damnation, but we also want our caretaker, like an idealized mother, to love us just the way we are—no matter how few books we have read, no matter how fat we are, no matter how much beer we drink on Saturday nights. We want another chance, and yet another chance, and yet another chance to learn to be good.

Milton's vision is not only starker. He is also, unquestionably, an arrant snob and aesthete. Beauty, among angels, is more than

skin deep. It is their badge, their uniform, their identity card. Satan
recognizes the archangel Uriel, "one of the sev'n / Who in God's
presence, nearest to his Throne / Stand ready at command and are
his Eyes," by his "radiant visage":

> His back was turn'd, but not his brightness hid;
> Of beaming sunny Rays, a golden tiar
> Circl'd his Head, nor less his Locks behind
> Illustrious on his Shoulders fledge with wings
> Lay waving round; on some great charge employ'd
> He seem'd, or fixt in cogitation deep.[13]

Intellect and reason are also hallmarks of the angelic host. When
Abdiel, infuriated by Satan's insubordination, "his own undaunted
heart explores," he contrasts his clear thinking with Satan's, which
he declares "Unsound and false":

> nor is it aught but just,
> That he who in debate of Truth hath won,
> Should win in Arms, in both disputes alike
> Victor: though brutish that contest and foul,
> When Reason hath to deal with force, yet so
> Most reason is that Reason overcome.[14]

Yet when Satan taunts Abdiel with what seems to be a perfectly
plausible observation,

> At first I thought Liberty and Heav'n
> To heav'nly Souls had been all one; but now
> I see that most through sloth had rather serve,
> Minist'ring Spirits, train'd up in Feast and Song;
> Such hast thou arm'd, the Minstrelsy of Heav'n,
> Servility with freedom to contend,

the angel "stern repli'd":

> Unjustly thou deprav'st it with the name
> Of *Servitude* to serve whom God ordains,
> Or Nature; God and Nature bid the same,
> When he who rules is worthiest, and excels
> Them whom he governs. This is servitude,
> To serve th' unwise, or him who hath rebell'd
> Against his worthier, and thine serve thee,
> Thyself not free, but to thyself enthrall'd.[15]

So intellect and reason get the angels no further down the path of knowledge than the message on the Parkman church sign got me: just obey; you'll be glad you did.

I'd like to say I've figured out how to make peace with these angelic explanations, but I haven't. At bottom, Milton's reasoning seems like nothing more than a parent's classic argument squelcher: "Because I said so!" It's a useful phrase, and I've employed it myself during long car rides and disputes about the importance of legible handwriting on homework. But then I've been arguing with children who, though they've had the bad luck to end up with a mother who will never buy them an ATV, at least get taken to the Harmony Fair's demolition derby every summer. And someday they'll grow up and most likely not buy ATVs for their children either. But that's as they see fit. Milton's angels worry me, not least because they suggest how far the poet was from comprehending the natural progression of patriarchy. His angels are boys in men's bodies, inhabitants of a static heaven where every "choice" they make centers on pleasing the father. Here, in our fallen world, every father was once a son—even Milton, though I'm not sure he wants me to know.

Ageless they are, these glorious angels; and ageless their poem. But Milton and I: we expand and dissolve and vanish; and that is the crux of our failures as imperfect minister, imperfect congregant.

Neither can adjust his rate of change—his expansions and contractions—for the other. Time shifts; great terrors align and realign our vision; we slumber in a narcotic quotidian haze. Yet far beyond our ken

> th' Angelic throng
> Disperst in Bands and Files thir Camp extend
> By living Streams among the Trees of Life,
> Pavilions numberless.[16]

There they stand—erect, eternal—though Milton and I cannot converse about them. But angels "seek not the praise of men." So silence may, after all, suffice.

7

Clear-Cuts

Immediate in a flame,
But soon obscur'd with smoke, all Heav'n appear'd,
From those deep-throated Engines belcht, whose roar
Embowell'd with outrageous noise the Air,
And all her entrails tore, disgorging foul
Thir devilish glut.

W HEN FINANCIAL ADVISERS, ex-college roommates, middle-aged attendees of poetry readings, and the like ask, usually in tones of disbelief, what possessed me to move to a hole in the wall like Harmony, I often find myself stammering, "It's quiet here," or "Land was cheap," or some similar reductive inanity. Such questions make me anxious. I fear that the spectacle of my everyday territory is liable, in an onlooker's eyes, to disintegrate into a strange and gothic absurdity. And I'm not wrong to fear. Most onlookers are primed for weirdness: either comic or sinister will do. Incest, overalls, and family feuds: along with tranquility, life à la *Ethan Frome* and *Cold Comfort Farm* are what the city-bred often expect from a country retreat.

Most educated Americans have become exquisitely remote from any sensuous interaction with the earth. I use *exquisite* here in the sense of both "intense" and "delicately elaborate"; for I think our distance from the soil is very nearly ceremonial. As well-heeled professionals, we are fixated on cleanliness, fitness, and organic frozen foods. We talk the go-green talk: "healthy ecosystem," "endangered wildlife," "clean air." But unless you count a refreshing bike ride through a national park or a fun weekend spent kayaking or cross-country skiing as exemplars of country life, most of us have almost no actual contact with the filth and heavy machinery that function alongside such "natural" pleasures—and in some cases control their very existence.

Thus arise an onlooker's peculiar, sometimes contradictory, but almost always Technicolor notions of rural character. As Thomas Hardy dryly noted, "it is only the old story that progress and picturesqueness do not harmonise." Yes, the country is a blessed retreat, a slice of Eden—"in narrow room Nature's whole wealth, yea more, / A Heaven on Earth"—preserved in Saran Wrap for the delectation of tired lawyers and stockbrokers as they slip their weary feet into ergonomically correct Birkenstocks and fire up the all-natural charcoal in the grill. But doesn't that pretty surface hide a seething nest of horrors?[1]

In their hunt for munitions powerful enough to defeat God, Satan and his fellow apostates go straight to nature, that raw and dreadful source.

> in a moment up they turn'd
> Wide the Celestial soil, and saw beneath
> Th' originals of Nature in thir crude
> Conception; Sulphurous and Nitrous Foam
> They found, they mingl'd, and with subtle Art,
> Concocted and adusted they reduc'd
> To blackest grain.[2]

Time falters on, yet assumptions linger. Milton, in his London bookroom, is not so far removed from contemporary ambivalence about the countryside, that unruly outback linking civilization and the wild. Even heaven, he tells me, conceals beneath its "fresh Flow'rets" "th' originals of Nature in thir crude / Conception." All-powerful God has not entirely erased nature's hideous forces; he has merely hidden them under a manicured lawn, green and rippling as a golf course, where Satan, "inspir'd / With dev'lish machination," mines their "hidd'n veins" to construct an angel-crushing missile.[3]

Throughout *Paradise Lost*, Milton has made it clear that he's suspicious of wildness, whether exemplified by beasts or personal volition. Paradise is nature tamed, a docile grove devoted to human and celestial comforts. When I think of Milton's heaven, I picture Kew, that stately pleasure garden, that masterpiece of manipulated beauty, unreal as a postcard. Yet there it stands, sturdy as a fairy palace, with its rhododendron alleys, its sweeping crocus moor, a regal monument to dirt in disguise. But if Kew is nature with a facelift, then heaven is Galatea spirited to flesh by her sculptor's kiss. Perfection basks in the light of its designer. So I'm perplexed by this small grey patch of uncertainty: why has the poet's God permitted wild, ugly, chaotic, foul-smelling nature to remain within the purview of heaven?

When the good angels first lay eyes on the massive catapult that Satan and his cohorts have constructed from heaven's underbelly, they seem more fascinated than frightened. Raw nature may be hideous, but technology is a strange and compelling novelty.

> Our eyes discover'd new and strange,
> A triple-mounted row of Pillars laid
> On Wheels (for like to Pillars most they seem'd
> Or hollow'd bodies made of Oak or Fir
> With branches lopt, in Wood or Mountain fell'd)

Brass, Iron, Stony mould, had not thir mouths
With hideous orifice gap't on us wide,
Portending hollow truce.[4]

It's no wonder they're confused. Technology is a miracle, a wondrous amalgam of material and intellect. Yet nature is so often both progenitor and prey of the machine, and pinpointing the nexus between the devilments of destruction and the civilized pleasures of paradise can become suddenly and ominously difficult.

Outside my house today, the cold air vibrates with a low, steady machine drone, punctuated with occasional crashes of steel and the rising whine of engines under stress. The Morrisons, owners of both the local garage and a logging business, are cutting a swath of forest half a mile away, on the other side of Grant Brook. As I trudge from woodshed to porch carrying firewood, I snuff up a familiar, pervading smell. It's not diesel, as one might have predicted from the noise. It's the aroma of hundreds of crushed fir, pine, and spruce trees: sharp, sugary, insidious as camphor or peppermint, riddling the breeze with a lifetime's supply of joyous Christmas spirit.

"Rose as in Dance the stately Trees" in Eden, but only lapsarian utility could teach us that a crushed conifer grove smells like heaven. Such complications—do I love this? do I hate this?—are rife in the nature versus machine debacle. For there's no easy side to take in this messy mix of desolation and pleasure. Shall I revile the Morrisons, owners of the bulldozers and skidders and pulp trucks that chew up the forest floor, crush rabbit dens and poison vernal pools, rewrite the skyline and erase acres of lanky, aging pines in the space of an afternoon? These same Morrisons are a family of sweet, shy men who've rescued me from more than one automotive pickle; whose garage smells charmingly of old coffee and spilled bar-and-chain oil—a slow-time place where I've often passed an hour perched on a cracked stool waiting for young Kyle or Ross to patch a tire or replace an alternator, *Orlando* or *War and Peace* on my lap, as various loggers on mysterious business wander through in their coveralls and discover, to their respectful embarrassment, that a woman is sitting at the parts counter . . . *and she's reading.*[5]

Shall I revile myself, carrying my armloads of firewood, which Tom has cut from trees in our own woods, using a chainsaw and a pickup, tearing up a few of our own forest paths, poisoning our silence? Shall I revile myself for writing about Milton, which requires pencils and paper that came into being thanks to their own complement of bulldozers, skidders, and pulp trucks?

Clearly the correct answer is yes. Neither our well-meaning niceness nor our financial, intellectual, or body-warmth requirements excuse our complicity in the injuries we inflict on nature. Yet like any carnivorous prowler, we're also helpless in the matter. As Hardy wrote, "it is too much to expect [people] to remain stagnant and old-fashioned for the pleasure of romantic spectators." When maintaining oneself *as* oneself is at stake, a patina of good intentions doesn't replace our deeper urge to survive intact—in whatever way we, as individuals, define survival. This is problematic, of course, not least because our safe and customary definitions of survival are profoundly invested in the habits, mores, histories, beauties, and technological know-how of Western civilization. Without a trace of irony, we transform refrigerators and telephones into bare necessities.[6]

Humanity's guilt-free enslavement of nature is nothing new, as Milton's rambling and gratuitous celebrations of celestial progress remind me. God's creation of earth, for instance, is wrought in bizarre, crypto-geological language that makes the Almighty sound like the Mad Alchemist of the Universe. Yet the scene is pure encomium, a hymn in praise of divine tinkering, of God's glorious production line churning out that useful commodity, nature.

His brooding wings the Spirit of God outspread,
And vital virtue infus'd, and vital warmth
Throughout the fluid Mass, but downward purg'd
The black tartareous cold Infernal dregs
Adverse to life; then founded, then conglob'd
Like things to like, the rest to several place
Disparted, and between spun out the Air,
And Earth self-balanc't on her Centre hung.[7]

So when people ask why I've chosen to live in Harmony, land of clear-cuts and "cursed Engines," I'm uneasy because I'm confused. If human hands have spoiled this place, yet they've also made it dear to me, even as they flush sewage into the brooks and fling Wal-Mart bags into roadside ditches. Being human, I cannot divorce myself from myself. As Carroll's Alice complains, "what is the use of a book . . . without pictures or conversations?" My analogue is "What is the use of a place without the people who live there?" It's a query that reflects my guilty, shifting, hierarchical affections for the place itself—pure sky, soil, animals, trees, stones—versus the people who pass their lives here drinking Diet Pepsi, fixing transmissions, driving the ambulance, boiling maple syrup, reading Harlequin romances, and singing along with AC/DC on the classic-rock station. It might be morally wrong, on a universal scale, to ask, "What is the point of nature *to me?*" But that doesn't make the question any less valid.[8]

In *Paradise Lost*, Milton's views about raw versus civilized nature are similarly conflicted; and more than once in the poem, his mixed feelings erupt into violence, generally at nature's expense:

Forthwith (behold the excellence, the power
Which God hath in his mighty Angels plac'd)
Thir Arms away they threw, and to the Hills
(For Earth hath this variety from Heav'n
Of pleasure situate in Hill and Dale)

> Light as the Lightning glimpse they ran, they flew,
> From thir foundations loos'ning to and fro
> They pluckt the seated Hills with all thir load,
> Rocks, Waters, Woods, and by the shaggy tops
> Uplifting bore them in thir hands.[9]

In this appalling scene, a battalion of good angels rips up "the seated Hills with all thir load" as if they're tearing out wall-to-wall carpeting and then hurls the jumbled, gutted surface of heaven at the rebel angels and their war machines. Not surprisingly, the bad guys are aghast.

> Amaze,
> Be sure, and terror seiz'd the rebel Host,
> When coming towards them so dread they saw
> The bottom of the Mountains upward turn'd,
> Till on those cursed Engines' triple-row
> They saw them whelm'd, and all thir confidence
> Under the weight of Mountains buried deep,
> Themselves invaded next, and on thir heads
> Main Promontories flung, which in the Air
> Came shadowing, and opprest whole Legions arm'd.[10]

There's something hideous about Milton's imagination here—something terrifying in his projection of the dire acts God permits from those who battle evil but also a dreadful revelation of divine (and possibly the poet's own) indifference to the intrinsic value of the natural world. "War seem'd a civil Game / To this uproar," says Milton, who never saw a news photo of the *Enola Gay*'s horrific aftermath. Yet though we know two cities were smashed, our images of Nagasaki and Hiroshima are primarily those of terrible human suffering, while the most vivid and shocking scenes of Milton's narrative of celestial *guerre à mort* devolve from these dreadful desecrations of landscape: "So Hills amid the Air encounter'd Hills / Hurl'd to and fro with jaculation dire." Although he does write of physical suffering, his descriptions of pain can be wooden and unconvincing and sometimes even absurd, as when Satan's forces shoot their giant catapult at the good angels in their "Adamantine" armor:

> chain'd Thunderbolts and Hail
> Of Iron Globes, which on the Victor Host
> Levell'd, with such impetuous fury smote,
> That whom they hit, none of thir feet might stand,
> Though standing else as Rocks, but down they fell
> By thousands, Angel on Arch-Angel roll'd.[11]

When I first encountered this passage, I laughed, of course. For readers brought up on Beckett and Kafka, there's nothing so refreshing as a comic interlude in the midst of dread; and *Paradise Lost* as Saturday morning cartoon is an irresistible tangent. There's a Loony Tunes exuberance to the vision: a battery of stiff angels, under the Almighty Bugs's detached and sardonic eye, tumbling into one another like a thousand stony bowling pins. But the more I think about it, the more the scene's goofiness disintegrates into a bizarre, even ominous, parody of agony. When contrasted with Milton's epic images of environmental destruction, "horrid confusion heapt / Upon confusion," mere pain, even among angels, is a petty side issue in the magnificent confrontation of right and wrong. For all its simplifications, defining *right* as "what God likes" and *wrong* as "what God doesn't like" allows the poet tremendous moral leeway. He doesn't have to automatically succumb to the hierarchical pressures of care—the human urge to disguise our preferences as altruism. At the same time he is clear-eyed about the wrongs we inflict by inventing such hierarchies to suit our personal and cultural predilections and desires.[12]

Thus, I can't help but admire the coldhearted bravery of Milton's attitude toward the hierarchical inconsequence of bodies versus landscape, especially when I consider how the rest of us humans so predictably rank our anxieties about suffering: (1) people, (2) furry animals, and (way down the list) prickly plants, poisonous mushrooms, and unappealing fauna such as mosquitoes and slugs. Yet his fascination with the idea of throwing a hill at Satan doesn't arise from any special affection for the natural world. Indeed, he seems to savor the image far too much. Anybody who really loved a plot of land would wail and weep at the prospect of tearing it up by the roots. Not Milton. He's grinning and howling and shaking his fist like old John Brown roaring into Harpers Ferry.

After poring over *Paradise Lost* word for word for the better part of two years (and I still haven't finished the damn thing), I've grown fond of Milton—his soft spot for beauty, his grief over both the human condition and his own flaws, his quick-witted curiosity and silly show-off book learning, his unabashed arrogance, his brilliant linear synthesis of music and image. But I know that, like certain contemporary zealots—those who believe, for instance, that murdering gynecologists is morally defensible—he'd condemn me to hang without a qualm. Nothing matters but the mission. And his God is similarly disengaged from the personal catastrophes of celestial war. Angels must be grievously wounded; hills must be torn up by the roots. You can almost see him shrug.

> and now all Heav'n
> Had gone to wrack, with ruin overspread,
> Had not th' Almighty Father where he sits
> Shrin'd in his Sanctuary of Heav'n secure,
> Consulting on the sum of things, foreseen
> This tumult, and permitted all, advis'd:
> That his great purpose he might so fulfil,
> To honor his Anointed Son aveng'd
> Upon his enemies, and to declare
> All power on him transferr'd.[13]

In Harmony today, the sun is shining, glinting off the softening snowbanks that line my driveway, highlighting muddy dog-nose smears on the windows. A fly bumps and hums lazily against my bedroom ceiling. Goldfinches hog the feeder, chasing chickadees off the perches, snapping their beaks at one another like aggravated shoppers. Outside in his garage workshop Tom is planing boards for the kitchen cabinets he's constructing for an organic grower who lives a few towns closer to civilization and apparently makes a fine living from hawking vegetables to university professors. The planer's howl mingles with the more distant whine of the Morrisons' chipper, which is shredding a mountain of leftover brush and branches, probably in hopes of selling them as pulp to a downriver paper mill. The birds—goldfinches, chickadees, nut-hatches, an occasional woodpecker or blue jay—seem indifferent to the racket, as do my hens, scrabbling enthusiastically among the freezer-burned strawberries I tossed them a few hours ago. Only the poodle is concerned. She barks periodically, nose to the wind, frizzy ears twitching. Perhaps she worries that the din portends the invasion of a giant land-sucking vacuum cleaner. She is not fond of vacuuming.

Why is the poodle the only creature within my ken who appears to be the least bit worried about the implications of this "infernal noise"? Perhaps it's more usual for creatures to ignore encroaching destruction—until they're destroyed, of course. Deer are drawn to the fresh, easy-to-negotiate undergrowth that springs up in a clear-cut; bears love a dump; and when "all Heav'n [goes] to wrack," God doesn't bat an eye. Of course he's perfectly safe from destruction himself; and it's always simpler to deal with chaos when you're "shrin'd in [a] Sanctuary . . . secure," whether that means a throne in heaven or the cab of a log skidder. To me, the howl of Tom's planer implies we'll cover this month's mortgage payment and maybe fix the Subaru's sagging suspension, if we don't blow his earnings on food and the electric bill. For creatures like the deer and myself, sidetracked by present-tense issues such as travel and dinner, destruction can have a cozy sound.[14]

And there's the lure, always, of believing that destruction doesn't matter. Everything can be mended. Seedlings will sprout; foul smoke will drift harmlessly away. When God transfers the war's generalship to "his Anointed Son," the Messiah, en route to victory, patches up heaven in a scant handful of lines:

> At his command the uprooted Hills retir'd
> Each to his place, they heard his voice and went
> Obsequious, Heav'n his wonted face renew'd,
> And with fresh Flow'rets Hill and Valley smil'd.[15]

This is the heaven we so often believe we possess on earth—a landscape "obsequious" and perennially forgiving. In a way, Milton's chilly yet evenhanded disregard for bodily and environmental suffering is easier to accept than my own exculpatory selfishness, the ease with which I overlook or forget my poisonous influence on the territory I call home, my half-hearted attempts to palliate guilt. Yet Milton's indifference is predicated on God's. As *Paradise Lost* reminds readers time and again, God doesn't care about anything—be it animal, plant, person, or angel—that does not specifically promote his formulations of universal righteousness. When we, as a species, internalize this directive and manipulate it toward our own mundane ends, we demonstrate, if nothing else, a glib imitation of divine power.

At the end of Book VI, the Messiah in "his fierce Chariot" drives inexorably toward victory, "Gloomy as Night," and "under his burning Wheels,"

> The steadfast Empyrean shook throughout,
> All but the Throne itself of God.

Yet instead of destroying the rebels, he chooses to "root them out of Heav'n":

> The overthrown he rais'd, and as a Herd
> Of Goats or timorous flock together throng'd
> Drove them before him Thunder-struck, pursu'd
> With terrors and with furies to the bounds
> And Crystal wall of Heav'n, which op'ning wide,
> Roll'd inward, and a spacious Gap disclos'd
> Into the wasteful Deep; the monstrous sight
> Struck them with horror backward, but far worse
> Urg'd them behind; headlong themselves they threw
> Down from the verge of Heav'n, Eternal wrath
> Burn'd after them to the bottomless pit.[16]

Out of sight, out of mind. A civilization's comfortable self-satisfaction accrues from such trivialities. The victorious angels, lauding their chief's decision to peel back the "Crystal wall of Heav'n" and chase the rebels into the "wasteful Deep," are perfectly content to ignore what they don't see. So are the goldfinches squabbling at my bird feeder. So are the weekend tourists, buzzing up Route 95 in their shiny Explorers, headed for a refreshing interaction with nature. And so am I, pretending to love the wild as I pervert it to suit my own purposes.

> Thus measuring things in Heav'n by things on Earth
> At thy request, and that thou mayst beware
> By what is past, to thee I have reveal'd
> What might else to human Race been hid.[17]

Life in the country is indeed a strange and gothic absurdity, beauty and brutality contorted into a semblance of heaven. "Harmony, Maine," a sentimental telemarketer once marveled to me. "How lovely it must be." Yes, it is lovely, a land of lakes and eagles and broad blue skies and diesel fumes and stumps; and it's not so different from heaven either. In his first great conflict with evil, the Messiah's instant response is to create "a spacious Gap," which he stuffs with satanic trash. "Hell at last / Yawning receiv'd them whole, and on them clos'd." And then the Messiah dusts off his hands and rides

> Triumphant through mid Heav'n, into the Courts
> And Temple of his mighty Father Thron'd
> On high; who into Glory him receiv'd,
> Where now he sits at the right hand of bliss.[18]

Sweep the devil under the rug, and we're all set for a happy dénouement. Except that *Paradise Lost* doesn't end here. Unlike most of us, Milton wasn't a sucker for "out of sight, out of mind." As Raphael reminds Adam, Satan "now is plotting how he may seduce / Thee also from obedience." Destruction has its consequences; and with a landfill seething underneath, even heaven's pure soil is laced with toxic waste.[19]

8

The Mystery of Sons

This day I have begot whom I declare
My only Son, and on this holy Hill
Him have anointed, whom ye now behold.

Unlike Milton and God, I am the mother of two boys.
And unlike those single-minded and ambitious fathers, I have not
suffered a son's death. These three differences—motherhood, a
pair of sons, and my boys' everyday physical presence—have vastly
influenced my moral and emotional comprehension of the world.
I have learned, for instance, that my life is not my own: I am the
handmaid of my children; I minister to their demands; I deny my
yearnings in service to theirs. Culturally this is a mother's role; but
while it is demeaning and self-destroying, it is also vivifying and
rigorous. Like strict training in any discipline, the self-negations
and hardships of raising children can, by means of honed boredom
and obsessive observation, set a mind at liberty.

Yet neither the ambiguities of motherhood nor the intricate relations between mothers and children interest Milton or Milton's God. *Paradise Lost* has no use for the quotidian spats and intimacies of family life—those bickering dialogues about eating what you've been served and washing with soap, that endless anthropomorphic commentary about the dog, a decade's worth of fervent backtalk about bedtime. For patriarchs such as Milton and God, love for an heir is a serious matter, endlessly vaunted and discussed yet, for all its pomp, arid and detached. This blinkered focus strikes me as terribly sad on a personal level (if one can use *personal* to describe God), but it is also central to the poem; for I think that a father's loss of his one son, whether foreseen or unexpected, whether as myth or as memory, lies at the heart of the tragedy of *Paradise Lost*, mirrored in the poem's rigid adherence to the doctrine of father as king as well as its idealized and distorted image of the father-son bond.

The constraints of biblical veracity meant that Milton had, to a certain degree, little choice in his characterizations. His God is indeed an Old Testament patriarch—tyrannical, unbending, and selfish—and Milton can perorate ad nauseam about the Almighty's relentless, controlling grip on the universe. But like many big talkers, the poet can be most revelatory when he is silent; and there's a gap in his exposition: how exactly do his windbag depictions of God the father of creation relate to his ambivalent and painful portraits of God the father of a son?

One can argue that the God of *Paradise Lost*, as the father to end all fathers, has spawned innumerable sons, notably his docile angels, his bad-boy apostate angels, and that dopy washout Adam. Yet he explicitly refers to the Messiah as his "only Son," himself comprehending some essential difference between *sons* as inferior servants and *son* as heir of a father's power and devotion. To me, this seems relevant to the anomaly of Milton's own fatherhood: he did indeed lose his only son, but his two daughters survived, only to become elements of his back story: meek amanuenses, mere girls, fringe characters in a long history of daughterly oppression.

Girls, however, are accustomed to living the back story; and probably any one of us can imagine what Milton's daughters might have been doing in the kitchen while he was groaning over *Paradise Lost* in his study: complaining about the lady next door, or maybe darning socks or shelling out broad beans or chasing the cat away from the stew meat. In short, they were doing what women have always done together in kitchens—talking and working and watching and listening. It's a familiar world to me; for with no brothers and a stay-at-home mother, I grew up in a cozy, girl-centered cocoon of paper dolls, chatter, baking, and ironing. Kitchen life is immersion in trivia, but it is also immersion in detail. The small transcends the grand: when you're frying an egg or caramelizing sugar, the compression of a minute matters considerably more than any epic battle; and the free-form talk that floats through a day spent boiling jam can raise the forsaken dead.

I was a daughter, and I expected to bear daughters. I never thought twice about it. So when I became the mother of sons, I was amazed and to a certain degree appalled. What did I know about boys? They had big feet and did stupid things like make fart noises in front of the teacher. Loud guitars seduced them like crows to road kill. They were mysterious, rude, grubby, and desperately charming, but how did you raise one?

According to my friend Jilline, God was testing my faith; otherwise, why would I have given birth to a baby who looked exactly like Edward G. Robinson? She herself had two younger brothers so was entitled to be flippant. And as I reminded myself during midnight diaper changes, hysterics over Hot Wheels cars, and

horrid tomato-sauce incidents, there's much historical prestige
connected to the bearing of sons. It was some comfort to consider
that, had I been unfortunate enough to be queen of England or a
T'ang dynasty concubine, Henry VIII would not have sliced off my
head and palace servitors would not have left my babies to starve
to death on a stony mountainside.

For I loved my sons in mysterious and unexpected ways. Though
I'd imagined motherhood to be an altruistic calling, I discovered
that, like other loves I'd undergone, whether for boyfriend or
great-aunt or Hereford heifer calf, attachment to my children was
linked to their attachment to me. Yet my sons' devotion was focused
and specific and thus deeply, helplessly heartrending. More than
anyone else on earth, they took me seriously. What I muttered
or dropped while I poured milk, how I smelled after a bath, the
winter texture of my hands: all of this mattered enormously to
them. And in turn my duties—feeding, carrying, dressing, wiping,
washing them—required an extrasensory, microscopic, obsessive
observation that nothing in my life had otherwise demanded. It
was dreadful. It was also exhilarating.

Nonetheless, the fundamental selfishness of my love for my
sons didn't diminish its terrors—in particular, the unarticulated
fear that by accident or evil, and perhaps because of my stupidity,
we would be torn apart. What if they die in a car crash because
I've been eating potato chips while driving? What if they burn
in hell because I haven't joined the church? Such fears, I think,
are endemic to parenthood, though we cannot always express or
recognize them and frequently cloak them in anger or bullying
dominance or self-lacerating melodrama. This, for instance, is how
God talks about his love for his son:

> O thou in Heav'n and Earth the only peace
> Found out for mankind under wrath, O thou
> My sole complacence![1]

It's as if Milton conceived of the Creator as the father of all father stereotypes—a passionate yet remote man, bitter, ranting, and lonely, who trudges his worn trail through history.

A father's dreams for his offspring tread a boulder-strewn route between self-pride and child-pride. Knowing full well that their daughters were desperate for independence and romance, both Patrick Brontë and Leslie Stephen nonetheless wheedled and waylaid and tormented them, unable to tolerate any adjustment in their familial bond. Such changes endanger a father's feudal control as well as the restorative comforts of a child's attention and admiration. But God himself does not hesitate to manipulate his beloved son in order to bolster his own pride, as in the following passage, when he hands off the task of creating earth with a commendation that is also a warning:

> And thou my Word, begotten Son, by thee
> This I perform, speak thou, and be it done:
> My overshadowing Spirit and might with thee
> I send along, ride forth, and bid the Deep
> Within appointed bounds be Heav'n and Earth,
> Boundless the Deep, because I am who fill
> Infinitude, nor vacuous the space
> Though I uncircumscrib'd myself retire,
> And put not forth my goodness, which is free
> To act or not, Necessity and Chance
> Approach not mee, and what I will is Fate.[2]

How often has love for children, and a longing for their love, driven family patriarchs into antagonism, histrionics, and manipulation? This sense of separation, of exile within the family, is a burden that men continue to carry, one that I sporadically glimpse even in Tom's interactions with our sons: a fraught, knife-edged pride and embarrassment; isolation entangled with communion. In the mornings, on their way out the door to school, our boys

always bumble up against me in their coats and boots and back-
packs for a good-bye kiss. But sometimes they forget to kiss Tom,
even when he's sitting at the table in front of them. I hate this and
usually make them stop and say good-bye to him. But do any of
them care about sharing good-bye kisses? I don't know. All three
accept their sliver of detachment without comment.

Mothers, of course, contend with their own burdensome stereotypes, which often feature us as doting flunkies of our children.
Sometimes we play the role of happy nursemaid, that soft-hearted
non-thinker who adores breastfeeding, cuddling, and singing
patty-cake. Sometimes our role takes the form of a more general-
ized beatification in which a mother's dutiful kindness and self-
denial ooze like a morphine drip into the lives of her offspring. In
either case, a woman's actual interaction with her actual child is
overshadowed by her place value in the maternal lineage. I think
here of a Sicilian fairy tale I recently read, which featured a queen
who longed for a child but gave birth instead to a rosemary plant.
Although she was surprised, the queen continued to behave like
a mother, planting the rosemary in a beautiful pot and watering it
with milk four times a day. Of course, being a fairy tale, the story
both fulfilled my expectations (by the end of the story, the rosemary
has turned into a dancing princess who marries the king of Spain)
and confused them: the queen's nephew takes a shine to the plant,
steals it from his aunt, and smuggles it onto his yacht, along with
a goat so he can keep up the milk regimen.[3]

Milton, however, avoided either messing with these parental
stereotypes or examining their consequences too carefully. The
trope of *Paradise Lost* is "do what your father tells you, and don't
ask questions," and Milton takes that order seriously. He is endlessly curious about how things work: What does an angel eat? Is
there a difference between day and night in heaven? Exactly how
are the apostates tortured in hell? But he remains obedient to the

ideal Old Testament hierarchies of human organization: man over woman, father over son, human over animal.

Yet real life never seems to fit the biblical ideal. Wives and children are always more opinionated than they ought to be, and sometimes the wolf conquers the hero. Milton knew this, of course. But his poem willed perfection to be otherwise. Like his descriptions of marriage, which he predicated on his unexamined, wistful notions of men as wise protectors of grateful, compliant women, his depictions of an ideal father-son love highlight his own human neediness. If his manicured paradise hints at his indifference to the rights of nature, his aching images of a perfect son, even when reduced to tag phrases and epithets, exude a real man's vulnerability to love and grief:

> on his right
> The radiant image of his Glory sat,
> His only Son.[4]

When I read Dickens's descriptions of good girls like Esther Summerson and Florence Dombey, I have similar feelings; for it seems to me that both men write fervently about imagined perfection in order to stanch their private wounds. But Milton preserves a formal distance between his characters that Dickens blithely overrides. For all their mutual love and admiration, God and his son do not cuddle, embrace, joke, or exhibit any behavior that hints at casual proximity and affection. This would be inappropriate in a high-flown epic featuring God and the Messiah. But why? Why does it demean the Creator's greatness to imagine him as a tender father who murmurs endearments to his son?

Though maternal stereotypes have damaged countless women's confidence in their private abilities and have crippled their public independence, even the worst forms of doting self-denial permit a mother to have close, affectionate, informal relations with her children. Nobody thinks less of the Virgin Mary because she pets and kisses her baby. But Milton doesn't seem to find this a particularly appealing attribute: the only lengthy scene of mother love in *Paradise Lost* portrays it as perversion. The incident takes place on the outskirts of hell, when Satan reacquaints himself with Sin, his daughter and former lover. Impregnated by their son Death, Sin has given birth to a pack of hellhounds,

> These yelling Monsters that with ceaseless cry
> Surround me, as thou saw'st, hourly conceiv'd
> And hourly born, with sorrow infinite
> To me, for when they list into the womb
> That bred them they return, and howl and gnaw
> My Bowels, thir repast; then bursting forth
> Afresh with conscious terrors vex me round,
> That rest or intermission none I find.
> Before mine eyes in opposition sits
> Grim *Death* my Son and foe, who sets them on,
> And me his Parent would full soon devour
> For want of other prey, but that he knows
> His end with mine involv'd: and knows that I
> Should prove a bitter Morsel, and his bane.[5]

Evidently, Milton did not care for babies. And it's not that I don't sympathize with him: I'm not a baby adorer myself. Perhaps if babies were less cute, more parents would kill them. But as it's taken me years to admit, love for a child doesn't mean you can't hate him too. Babies are indeed a torment, howling and gnawing at our bowels, devouring their parents for want of any other prey. Milton recognized the hate, without a doubt. What he didn't comprehend is hate's hair-shirt role in forging our bonds with our children.

Right now I'm fretting over the fact that I have so little time to myself. If only I had an entire day alone, I could write a masterpiece. If only I didn't have to quit writing mid-thought to race down to the cellar and stuff another load of mud-sopped pants into the washing machine. Or drive twenty-five miles in a sleet storm so Paul can bash out "Für Elise" on the piano. Or miss a day of writing while James pukes all over the couch. I hate all these things; at moments I hate them passionately. But as events, they're more than Erma Bombeck–style anecdotes of family life or fodder for aggravated telephone calls to my own mother. They *are* life. They subdue me; they override me; they excoriate me. Puking is more important than writing. Without my sons, how would I ever have learned this?

Of course, Milton's particular brand of greatness is predicated on precisely the opposite belief: writing is far, far more important than puking. No baby ever got the chance to spit up on his shoulder. Probably not many spit up on Dickens's shoulder either, but mostly because he was too busy transferring the spectacle to paper. I think Dickens did believe that writing was less important than puking. Writing just happened to be his obsession. But Milton had zero interest in the charms and irritations of childhood. God's only son arrives in heaven as an adult, conjured up without feminine interference and ready for command at a moment's notice. When the Creator announces, "This day I have begot whom I declare / My only Son," he's not celebrating the birth of a descendant but his own massive strength and dominance:

> your Head I him appoint;
> And by my Self have sworn to him shall bow
> All knees in Heav'n, and shall confess him Lord.[6]

As a believer in Christian obedience, Milton needed to delineate a God who is truly almighty; but unfortunately the poet's workbox was English, a language so impregnated with human-derived word choice, image, and metaphor that describing a spirit as a spirit is practically impossible. Faced with these limitations,

Milton chose to paint God as the Big Man who wears the crown of both tyrant and philosopher king, often at the same time. As the Creator informs the angels, under his son's "great Vice-gerent Reign [they shall] abide"

> United as one individual Soul
> For ever happy: him who disobeys
> Mee disobeys, breaks union, and that day
> Cast out from God and blessed vision, falls
> Into utter darkness, deep ingulft, his place
> Ordain'd without redemption, without end.
>   So spake th' Omnipotent, and with his words
> All seem'd well pleas'd, all seem'd, but were not all.[7]

To me, that final line is most indicative of Milton's descriptive dilemma. The hint of discomfort, which eventually explodes into celestial war, is here the blister that also rubs the fabulist. How do you write about a man who is not a man?

Milton's solution was to write about God in superhuman (and therefore ultimately human) terms while simultaneously undermining God's persistent manlike characteristics. In the case of the father-son conundrum, he endeavored to eliminate both sex and childhood from the picture. I can only guess that both arenas in some way implied a weakness that the poet was unwilling to delegate to God. Sex is an interesting choice; for as the Adam and Eve idyll makes clear, Milton thought physical love was an excellent and enjoyable benefit of ideal marriage. I suppose it was too sloppy for God, not to mention requiring a lady's presence in the story, which was neither biblically feasible nor a comfortable narrative prospect, given Milton's commitment to the solemn joys and duties of marriage partners. It's perfectly within character for Satan to have a one-night stand, but God's wife would have to be a permanent fixture—a problem that leads to the childhood complication.

Childhood without motherhood. This was, for a period of Milton's life, his everyday hell. According to the chronology that appears in my edition of *Paradise Lost*, his daughter Anne was born in October 1648, his son John in March 1651. On May 2, 1652, his daughter Deborah was born. Three days later his wife Mary died. And a month after that his year-old son died. The intense and complex miseries of this situation, even for a sensible, everyday man, are hardly possible to enumerate. For a man such as Milton—a patriarch who deeply disliked babies and household fuss and had untenable preconceptions about paternal love and duty—dealing practically and temperamentally with this string of losses must have made composing *Paradise Lost* feel like a stroll in the sunshine. He had probably never picked up a baby in his life, let alone noticed what any of his children were eating or wearing, whether or not they could use the privy, what made them cry or laugh, or how many hours they slept each night. And now he was solely responsible for the survival of two small daughters. Under such circumstances, what exactly was he mourning? The death of his wife? Or being left in the lurch? With the mother of the house dead, the quick loss of his son may have been a practical relief as much as a tragedy.[8]

But these afflictions were God's will; and Milton's Puritan convictions required him to accept them meekly, along with the anger, relief, guilt, and grief that were shackled to his burdens and losses. Milton hoped that *Paradise Lost* would "justify the ways of God to men." But perhaps he also hoped to justify the ways of God to himself, as both a representative man and a faulty, unruly, suffering individual. These collisions—between selfish, driven creator and obedient subject; between arrogant intellectual and baby-laden widower; between celestial poet and common sinner—seem crucial to the frozen, bewildering, submissive, ranting interchanges between father and son in heaven: "Effulgence of my Glory, Son belov'd"; "O Father, O supreme of heav'nly Thrones." Did Milton try, in these characterizations, to imagine a love and a meekness he could not sustain on earth? If so, the attempt is often laced with belligerence, as in the Son's response to God's order to assume generalship of the celestial war:

> This I my Glory account,
> My exaltation, and my whole delight,
> That thou in me well pleas'd, declar'st thy will
> Fulfill'd, which to fulfil is all my bliss.
> Sceptre and Power, thy giving, I assume
> And gladlier shall resign, when in the end
> Thou shalt be All in All, and I in thee
> For ever, and in mee all whom thou lov'st;
> But whom thou hat'st, I hate, and can put on
> Thy terrors, as I put thy mildness on,
> Image of thee in all things.[9]

It's rank invention for me to puzzle over these biographical connections, but I do so because I recognize the urge to splinter my own wretched behaviors—selfishness, guilt, jealousy, impatience—into mosaic bits and then reassemble them into multiple portraits that are not myself but a sort of flayed exhumation of myself. A few years ago I took to writing poems that faked the first-person, it's-all-about-me point of view. I featured the *I* as a poem's emotional centerpiece but either entirely invented the situation or knitted unrelated actual events into a fictional scenario. Though it was a relief and an interesting intellectual challenge to remove my own *I* from the limelight while participating in the surprises and manipulations of emotional revelation, I also discovered that such pretense only goes so far. To begin with, most readers (as well as many poets and editors of literary magazines) see poetry as a kind of hepped-up approach to diary writing. They assume that *I* equals *poet*. This is tiresome but understandable, given humanity's hunger for gossip, whether as art or talk-show fodder. But more important to me as a creator, the voices I invented in these poems never turned out to be entirely new people. I could falsify the situation, but somehow I kept turning up anyway.

With omniscient narrative, it's easier to forget that the poet is part of the poem. Yet even though the *I*'s stridency may fade into a more various clamor, the artist still paws through his own junkyard for material. Milton's junkyard was piled with riches—with ancient knowledge, with crystalline rhythm and jeweled metaphor, with stamina and belief and bravery—and those lavish gifts carried him, a mere mortal, even unto the reaches of heaven:

> Up led by thee
> Into the Heav'n of Heav'ns I have presum'd,
> An Earthly Guest, and drawn Empyreal Air,
> Thy temp'ring.[10]

But like anyone else's, his junkyard was also a clutter of faults and misperceptions and unreasonable longings. And no one has more misperceptions and unreasonable longings than a parent.

> And thou my Word, begotten Son, by thee
> This I perform, speak thou, and be it done:
> My overshadowing Spirit and might with thee
> I send along, ride forth, and bid the Deep
> Within appointed bounds be Heav'n and Earth.[11]

When it comes to our children, who among us is innocent of such vast absurdity? A son is a father's second chance: go forth, my child, and do what I haven't done myself. At the same time, the father is the power, the source, the wisdom from which the bright-eyed child springs. That's the dream. But in truth our sons are slippery fish, leaping recklessly from their parents' grasp into their own uncharted seas. Every Frankenstein has his monster, and that monster is his son.

Somehow this knowledge is easier to grasp now that I have two sons. For it briefly seemed possible that my oldest boy, James, would be an only child. Tom was none too keen on having another baby. This one is already too hard, was his best explanation. I thought this reasoning was specious since I was mopping up most of the mess. But in retrospect I know he was concerned about more than double loads of diapers and unpayable college tuition. James *was* too hard. The intensity of his gaze through the crib bars was frightening. We were his prey, in his gunsights night and day—snack time or bath time, sandbox or swing. He digested the workings of our minds. He demanded that we retrofit the world to his specifications: "Turn my eyes red." "Dig up gold." There was no escape. He expected too much of us. And we, in turn, expected too much of him. Every crayon scribble, every cleverly misused word signified . . . what? We didn't have an answer for "what?" but nonetheless his future hovered over us like a storm crow.

The birth of our second son, Paul, completely disrupted this obsessive vision. It was like switching from a magnifying glass to a kaleidoscope. Now I looked at two magnificently disparate boys: extra tall or extra short, goofy hair or glasses, crazy about duct tape or crazy about rocks, a shouter or an arguer, a maker of truck noises or a radio mimic. And the boys looked at each other, turning away now and then to watch me, to watch Tom, sometimes as a pair, sometimes separately. As they've grown, our mutual perceptions have splintered and fused and mirrored and distorted. The life of a family is vivid chaos, even in separation. Paul crouches by the radio all afternoon, intoning Red Sox play-by-plays, singing along with every Giant Glass and Hammond Lumber commercial. James whistles tunelessly as he hot-glues wine corks into a log-cabin-style replica of the Tower Bridge. Tom reads "The Heart of Darkness."

I fry sausage. Our isolations fracture and intersect, in confusion, in annoyance, in tenderness.

But Milton's son died young.

Paradise Lost does not primarily concern itself with the tale of Jesus the man. Yet the Son's voluntary death shadows the poem, foretold both narratively and in more subtle revelations of grief. In Book III, pleading clemency for mankind's sin, the Messiah declares to his father, "on me let Death wreck all his rage." Imagine hearing your son speak such terrible words. Strangely enough, I can.[12]

As the mother of a nine-year-old who stomps royally around the house bellowing a tune he calls "The Happy Fields of Conquer-Land," I'm accustomed to mythological bravado. The Son's assertion is incorporeal, impossible to scan as realistic adult speech; yet its matter-of-fact jaunty heroism—its solid jump-rope rhythm, its words-of-one-syllable vocabulary—is surprisingly childlike. The Messiah might be a fairy-tale prince, girding on his sword to face the dragon. His jauntiness doesn't last, of course. Being Milton's creation, his tone usually inclines toward liturgical gloom:

> life for life
> I offer, on mee let thine anger fall;
> Account me man; I for his sake will leave
> Thy bosom, and this glory next to thee
> Freely put off, and for him lastly die.[13]

Yet in this brief space, in half a throwaway line, a real son inhabits *Paradise Lost*—real because fantasy and sweet bravado are a young boy's shining sword, his swaggering defense against the fearful unknown. And the Messiah, though he looks like a full-grown prince, really was born yesterday.

Such small linguistic accidents make Milton's grief palpable, though he says nothing about himself or his son, though he tarts up the ambiguities of affection as pompous paternal control and smirking filial obeisance. His son died young, but his daughters lived on, becoming real girls and then real women who served and irritated and enraged their aggravating, obnoxious, brilliant father. The demands of his material—God the Father, Christ the Son—gave him permission to tell lies as well as truths. No daughters necessary in the story of heaven. Well, maybe Satan can have a daughter. But she has to be awful.

Yet blind reverence exacts its own toll. Milton the evangelist, Milton the voice of an angry God, found himself licensed to render not only perfection—the ideal kinship of father and son—but also anguish, that celestial melodrama, which nonetheless allotted him, quietly, invisibly, room for plain human grief.

> Father, thy word is past, man shall find grace;
> And shall grace not find means, that finds her way,
> The speediest of thy winged messengers,
> To visit all thy creatures, and to all
> Comes unprevented, unimplor'd, unsought?[14]

9

"Celestial Song"

Forth flourish'd thick the clust'ring Vine, forth crept
The smelling Gourd, up stood the corny Reed
Embattl'd in her field: and the humble Shrub,
And Bush with frizzl'd hair implicit.

AFTER SPENDING roughly two years copying out *Paradise Lost* word for word, I am now far less sure about what constitutes a good line of poetry than I was before I started the project. Why is a certain conglomeration of words termed beautiful or ugly, silly or satirical, dull or impassioned? How do preconceptions about the aesthetics of language and what constitutes an acceptable style of expression influence my judgment?

As designated great art, *Paradise Lost* has received canonical tenure; it's been promoted to a mahogany case in a locked upstairs room. Criticism of the poem no longer involves crowing or complaint but has graduated to scholarly weightlifting. It's hard to remember that the poem may have existed in a present-tense world of muddled praise and jealousy and ignorance. It's hard to conceive that it ever had a plain, undemanding, ignorant new reader, a middle-aged man, perhaps, who opened the book by accident as he sat warming his feet by his cousin's fire, thoughtlessly picking up the epic lying next to him on the settle as I might pick up some *New York Times* bestseller left on a dentist's magazine table: twiddling it between my hands, examining the cover, randomly cracking it open at page 63, and dipping into unexpected waters.

Paradise Lost has no such readers today. High school teachers may assign a section or so to bewildered or uninterested college-prep students, and doctoral candidates may see it as relevant fodder for a dissertation or a journal article. An optimistic bookworm might tackle a few pages in hopes of assuaging some indefinite yearning for knowledge. But who finds it spread-eagled on a dentist's magazine table or bookmarked with a towel next to a public swimming pool? Though it once lived a physical life, the poem as an object has no free commerce with our daily world.

Because interactions with *Paradise Lost* have been reduced to either the rarefied commentary of specialized readers or slack-jawed student indifference, I find it difficult to trust my judgment of the work as a construction or my motives for liking or disliking it. I can respond like a high school sophomore, distilling my distrust of strangeness and complexity into eye rolling or "Yuck." I can retreat to an easy cosmopolitan cynicism, in which ridicule masquerades as world-weary cleverness ("The Epic Treadmill, or Famous Bores in History"). Like *Middlemarch*'s Mr. Casaubon, I can burrow away at obscure references and mythological minutiae, peering through my dusty microscope at "*Eden* over *Pontus*, and the Pool / *Maeotis*, up beyond the River *Ob*." Like a half-baked literary evangelist, I can extol the poem's cosmic scope, its magnificent characterization of evil, of Satan "full of anguish driv'n," "bent / on Man's destruction, maugre what might hap / Of heavier on himself." But can I ask, "Is this line good? Is it bad? Is there a difference? Does it matter?"[1]

There's the shyness I feel as an inferior artist, of course. For there's no question that *Paradise Lost* is a miracle, a shape-shifting behemoth, a universe; and like Adam before his maker, I'm overwhelmed by Milton, who "Surpassest far my naming":

> How may I
> Adore thee, Author of this Universe,
> And all this good to man, for whose well being
> So amply, and with hands so liberal
> Thou hast provided all things.

But his epic is also littered with what contemporary poetry has coached me to believe are verbal infelicities, including clunky repetitions ("And every creeping thing that creeps the ground"), lack of variation (such as two lines in a row starting with "Or"), ridiculous syntax ("*Adam*, from whose dear side I boast me sprung"), as well as numbers of inadvertently comic descriptors ("Bush with frizzl'd hair implicit").[2]

It may be counterintuitive, given Milton's reputation for stately grandeur and labyrinthine syntax, to call these constructions unselfconscious; yet their clumsiness in the midst of pomp strikes me as peculiarly innocent. "Forth crept / The smelling Gourd, up stood the corny Reed": what could be sillier; what sweeter? Innocence is not a word generally associated with Milton, yet how else can I account for such rambunctious verbal sloppiness? It has the purity of youth, reckless as an elbowed glass of milk. And it charms me. For in a poem the size of *Paradise Lost*, how could the poet avoid those moments of tumbling invention, when words careened onto the page like screeching monkeys? I picture him bouncing up from his chair and waving his arms around, while his secretary-daughter hunches down on her stool in hopes of not getting slapped.

Milton's language is particularly impulsive in his long explanations of scientific wonders and natural history, as in Book VII, when he takes us through the six days of creation. Here he describes the first birds hatched on earth (and apparently the egg came before the chicken):

> Meanwhile the tepid Caves, and Fens and shores
> Thir Brood as numerous hatch, from th' Egg that soon
> Bursting with kindly rupture forth disclos'd
> Thir callow young.[3]

I haven't forgotten the shifting inexactitudes of language. In the poet's time "callow young" very likely connoted something substantially different from "pimple-faced kid." But what about "bursting with kindly rupture"? Was that line ever not funny? What possibly could have possessed Milton to pair "kindly" and "rupture"? The effect is jarring and slapstick, with an aura of accident, as if he'd been playing with a magnetic poetry kit.

I suppose humor depends, to a large degree, on one's expectations of a work; and it doesn't seem likely that anyone has ever expected a good laugh from a Bible-sized poem about humanity's fall from divine grace. Milton himself certainly had somber expectations: in the lugubrious opening lines of Book I, he glowers at his reader like a dyspeptic schoolmaster, ready to smack the first giggler with a yardstick as he invokes God's "aid to [his] advent'rous Song,"

> That with no middle flight intends to soar
> Above th' *Aonian* Mount, while it pursues
> Things unattempted yet in Prose or Rhyme.

And the dense, portentous tone of much of *Paradise Lost*—"Those Notes to Tragic," as Milton terms his moody, heavy style—is enough to make most readers collapse into word coma, where every subject seems to be identically important and all the details of sound and language melt, "with long and tedious havoc," into a waste of gluey orange cheese sauce.[4]

Yet even in word coma, how can you overlook this scene? Who knew that the first mammals exploded out of Eden's virgin soil like landmines?

> The grassy Clods now Calv'd, now half appear'd
> The Tawny Lion, pawing to get free
> His hinder parts, then springs as broke from Bonds,
> And Rampant shakes his Brinded mane; the Ounce,
> The Libbard, and the Tiger, as the Mole
> Rising, the crumbl'd Earth above them threw
> In Hillocks; the swift Stag from under ground
> Bore up his branching head; scarce from his mould
> *Behemoth* biggest born of Earth upheav'd
> His vastness: Fleec't the Flocks and bleating rose,
> As Plants.[5]

Nevertheless, I sometimes think I'm the only person in history who's ever laughed at *Paradise Lost*. In fact, I sometimes think I'm the only person in the world who's ever read it. Neither of these assertions is true, of course. Yet copying out the entire enormous, endless, complicated poem is a lonely task partly because living in Milton's mind is a lonely task. I ask myself, "Didn't he crack even a tiny smile after intoning 'The grassy Clods now Calv'd'?" And I think he didn't. I think he had no idea that any part of this scene was funny—not the "Tawny Lion" with his "hinder parts" stuck in the dirt, not the crowd of noisy woolly sheep sprouting "as Plants." Part of my tenderness toward the man arises from his solemn ignorance of the trivial powers of his tools: he oozed classical scholarship, forged an epic to rival Homer's, and in Satan created one of the greatest characters in literature. But he didn't comprehend that "the Tiger, as the Mole / Rising" deflates the tiger's nobility faster than a thumbtack on a queen's throne.

Of course, Milton isn't the only painfully serious poet in history. Virgil's *Aeneid* doesn't angle for laughter. Neither do *Beowulf* or the Bible, for that matter. By and large, the authors of epics are humorless. If comedy intrudes, it arrives accidentally and sometimes embarrassingly in snatches of "unpremeditated Verse." When we laugh at passages in *Great Expectations* and *Ulysses* and *Tristram Shandy*, we're fully aware that the writers expect us to laugh. There's nothing unpremeditated about the humor in *The Rape of the Lock*. But Milton doesn't expect me to laugh at him. He would be mortified, and also angry, to learn that some insouciant New World female had poked fun at his version of the sixth day of creation. So if I occasionally find myself imagining I've founded a Milton cult-of-one, I recognize, too, that I'm not so much an acolyte as a fond yet constantly exasperated daughter-in-law. That imagined familial bond loosens the reins of scholarship and respect: I can laugh at the poet but love him regardless. Yet I do so at the risk of offending his reputation, his earned greatness, his intentions. It is no small crime to belittle a life's work.[6]

Thus, what I feel when faced with a clutch of young birds, who "soaring th' air sublime / With clang despis'd the ground," is a complicated admixture of amusement at the inappropriate "clang"; embarrassment for the poet, blithely dead to the issue for all these years; and shame at having been sidetracked from honoring a great poet to sneering at a single ugly word. This seems, on one level, considerable overreaction to "clang." Yet I think my squirmy doubts illustrate the way in which contemporary experts—critics, teachers, ambitious practitioners—tend to critique a poem as a conglomeration of aesthetic parts rather than a striving, searching, living, ambiguous whole. I don't say that a beetle-browed focus on minute aspects of rhythm or language is wrong. But art is great not because it is perfect but because it can override its own blunders; and in Milton's case the sheer torrent of words was the poem's propulsion, as if "clang" were a necessary station-stop en route to the sublime. For the lines continue:

> there the Eagle and the Stork
> On Cliffs and Cedar tops thir Eyries build:
> Part loosely wing the Region, part more wise
> In common, rang'd in figure wedge thir way,
> Intelligent of seasons, and set forth
> Thir Aery Caravan high over Seas
> Flying, and over Lands with mutual wing
> Easing thir flight; so steers the prudent Crane
> Her annual Voyage, borne on Winds; the Air
> Floats, as they pass, fann'd with unnumber'd plumes.[7]

This glorious evocation of migration is itself akin to a flock of birds: the words join and take wing; "the Air / Floats as they pass, fann'd with unnumber'd plumes"; each syllable leaps unerringly into a pattern of sound that is also a pattern of sight and of meaning. If Milton had stopped to fuss over "clang," would he have maintained enough momentum to create such beauty?

The momentum of poetry is not something I hear much about, nor do I especially note it in the poems I come across in journals or classrooms, except insofar as it affects the basic structural klutziness of all new writers. The bonded momentum of sound, image, shape, and tale that so infects Coleridge's and Shakespeare's and Whitman's best work is not a modern poetic construct, partly because it requires a poet to ride out a riff that invites accident and error. Ginsberg aspired to such poetry and occasionally touched the hem of its garment; but like so many Whitman imitators, he was diverted into careless bluster rather than carried aloft by the rushing-river experience of writing as the concrete enactment of thought and emotion. Technically conscientious poets—those whom we might have expected to model themselves on Milton or Shakespeare or Coleridge—have in large part retreated to anxiety and bloodless perfectionism, where every word counts but no one knows exactly what it counts for.

There's a fine line between linguistic precision and fear of discovery, and a predilection for haiku or Williams-style compression may have little to do with verbal economy. Who invented that "less is more" catchphrase anyway? Not John Milton. And why do so many writers take it to heart? A lack of ambition or inspiration; the allure of aphoristic tidiness; boredom or dead ends or distraction or exhaustion. . . . Whatever the reason, under the guise of economy, too many poems ax the quest of poetry: to surprise ourselves into saying what we didn't know we knew. Verbal economy doesn't mean using the fewest words possible. It means writing everything you need to write as well as you can write it. This doesn't require honed perfection but relentless attention, and by that definition Milton was the most economical of writers. By sheer will and perseverance, he "calculate[d] the Stars, how they will wield / The mighty frame, how build, unbuild, contrive."[8]

But as he himself noted,

> The skill of Artifice or Office mean,
> Not that which justly gives Heroic name
> To Person or to Poem. Mee of these
> Nor skill'd nor studious, higher Argument
> Remains, sufficient of itself to raise
> That name.[9]

Milton's greatness relies on more than economy; for as a technician, he pushed poetry beyond beauty or storytelling into an active revelation of thought, with all its twists and turns and backsliding and discoveries.

Consider this passage, when Satan in the guise of a toad perverts Eve's innocent dreams,

> Assaying by his Devilish art to reach
> The Organs of her Fancy, and with them forge

Illusions as he list, Phantasms and Dreams,
Or if, inspiring venom, he might taint
Th' animal spirits that from pure blood arise
Like gentle breaths from Rivers pure, thence raise
At least distemper'd, discontented thoughts,
Vain hopes, vain aims, inordinate desires
Blown up with high conceits ingend'ring pride.[10]

Workshopped, the passage would suffer. "Pure blood" followed by "Rivers pure" may be a small matter, but some classroom complainer would surely point out that the repetition doesn't carry the rhythmic and sonic weight of "vain hopes, vain aims." Still, heaviest criticism would fall, I think, on Milton's easy deployment of undefined abstractions: those "discontented thoughts," those "high conceits ingend'ring pride."

Because I love this passage, I'm inclined to embrace these lines with a full heart and toss piddly infelicities to the wind. But I did notice "pure Blood" followed by "rivers Pure," and I did question it. So does that make me a pedant? Or does it make me a philistine?

"Examples! examples!" we are taught. "Keep poetry in the world!" And so we should. Yet there are worlds and there are worlds, and this is the land of "Phantasms and Dreams," where abstraction rules, where "inordinate desires" are as weighty and illusory as Satan's coaxing voice. The passage reveals the "Organs of [Eve's] Fancy" with marvelous accuracy because the poet relaxes into his language, ignores its fussy instructions, allows it to lift him up, like water or air, and carry him on a ripple of syntax and image and adjective-noun dreaminess into Eve's vulnerable sleeping brain.

AT THE BEGINNING of Book VII, Milton himself steps up from the shadows and sings a brief bardic lay about his frustrations and desires as a poet. It's an odd digression, unexpected, appearing in the middle of the poem, even in the middle of a conversation; and by the time I realize this is Milton talking, he's already directed me to Raphael and Adam and the story of creation. He addresses his lay to Urania, the Greek muse of astronomy, though he calls on "the meaning, not the Name," instead reinventing her as "Heav'nly born":

> Thou with Eternal Wisdom didst converse,
> Wisdom thy Sister, and with her didst play
> In presence of th' Almighty Father, pleas'd
> With thy Celestial Song.[11]

A woman as representative of eternal wisdom? This is shocking enough, considering Milton's crabby animadversions to Eve's powers of intellect. ("Not capable her ear / Of what was high," and she'd rather prune her "Fruits and Flow'rs" than sit around listening to Adam gab with the angels.) But Milton goes so far as to plead with this female, and what he pleads for is the gift of pedestrian poetry:

> Up led by thee
> Into the Heav'n of Heav'ns I have presum'd,
> An Earthly Guest, and drawn Empyreal Air,
> Thy temp'ring; with like safety guided down
> Return me to my Native Element:
> Lest from this flying Steed unrein'd, (as once
> *Bellerephon*, though from a lower Clime)
> Dismounted, on th' Aleian Field I fall
> Erroneous there to wander and forlorn.[12]

It's as if Milton, for all his self-confidence, has found himself forced to admit that the sublime is not, after all, his natural element. "More safe I Sing with mortal voice," he tells the muse, though being Milton, he can't resist decorating his humility with a trumpet blast. His voice may be mortal, but it's "unchang'd / To hoarse or mute." Don't expect false modesty from a shaman, and who do you think taught Whitman how to sing? Nevertheless, Milton does acknowledge that his talents are earthbound. Moreover, he's not sorry about it. He may grumble and complain and demand a better crowd of admirers ("still govern thou my Song / *Urania*, and fit audience find, though few. / But drive far off the barbarous dissonance / Of *Bacchus* and his Revellers"), yet he begs her not to fail him "who thee implores."[13]

Why did a return to everyday verse matter so much to the poet? And why did he decide this transitory invocation was important to include in the poem? As a segue between Raphael's story of heaven and his story of earthly creation, the passage allows Milton to brazenly position himself between heaven and earth. Yet he's homesick for earth; he's afraid of heaven; he's pleading to leave. He may be a Christian apologist in theme, but in poetic temperament he's a man, consumed with curiosity about geography and naked women and the composition of brimstone. And it's here—in his inquisitive, questing, flexible line; the foolish words that trip off his tongue; his eager adventuring into his own mind—that I discover some modicum of comfort. For I have a right to laugh at or linger over a poet who would rather be an ignorant artist than an angel. Ignorance may be the opposite of knowledge, but it's also innocence. What joy it must have been to know nothing, all the while unfurling *Paradise Lost*, that trove of nothing, from the shadows of his brain.

10

"What Harmony or True Delight?"

Tell me, how may I know him, how adore,
From whom I have that thus I move and live,
And feel that I am happier than I know.

Even here in central Maine—country of junked trailers and gravel pits, tattoo parlors and poisoned rivers; this "conflagrant mass" blotting the white man's biography of success—I live in an Eden of sorts. Perhaps it's true that "some Blood more precious must be paid for Man," but my neighbors and I nonetheless believe that no one will chop off our hands at dawn or disembowel our babies before our eyes. Never in memory has our town succumbed to smallpox or plague; and though our wells sometimes go dry in August, they always replenish in the autumn rains. "In mean estate [we] live moderate." We possess, according to the lessons of history, happy lives.[1]

Yet if one assumes happiness to imply a quiescent awareness of felicity and contentment, none of us is particularly happy. I'm not the only person who plans ahead for a wonderful Christmas—baking brandy-laced fruitcakes, decorating the piano with miniature snowy houses, purchasing magic tricks and fake mustaches for my sons—but spends the holiday shuffling from window to window, staring into the bleached landscape of a bare-ground December, burdened with that heavy, napless brooding common to a day without purpose. I don't know what I want, but I know I don't have it.

> Myself I then perus'd, and Limb by Limb
> Survey'd, and sometimes went, and sometimes ran
> With supple joints, as lively vigor led;
> But who I was, or where, or from what cause,
> Knew not.[2]

Discontent: it's one more stupid, obstinate failing of humanity, as anyone who's read *Madame Bovary* or "Dear Abby" can verify. But for the most part, stories of other people's unhappiness are strikingly useless paths to self-improvement. How many readers become happier and more contented after spending an evening with Heathcliff or the Ancient Mariner? Not one, I daresay. Yet I don't think that transmitting effective lessons in self-improvement mattered much to either Brontë or Coleridge, who wrote to explicate their own internal hells rather than to save humankind. The man who concocted *Paradise Lost* had a more suasive string of fish to fry.

"To speak I tri'd, and forthwith spake." Milton, that tireless student of the human condition, surely recognized by middle age that exhorting people to be happy or good or obedient was like spitting into a stiff wind. But as a missionary poet, he nonetheless found himself wading into the noxious puddles of pedantic argument, a class of writing I've always found difficult to stomach. I can't imagine that aligning himself with such "hideous gabble" was good for his temper. As he himself once complained, "what pleasure can there possibly be in the petty disputations of sour old men.... Many a time, when the duties of tracing out these petty subtleties for a while has been laid upon me, when my mind has been dulled and my sight blurred by continued reading ... how often have I wished that instead of having these fooleries forced upon me, I had been set to clean out the stable of Augeas again."[3]

"But the voice of God / To mortal ear is dreadful"; and though I agree that mucking out a barn can often seem more instructive, and certainly more refreshing, than combing through "the petty disputations" of this particular sour old man, I sympathize with Milton nonetheless, mostly because his hope that a giant bossy poem might repair the errors of human nature seems so brave and loony.

> O goodness infinite, goodness immense!
> That all this good of evil shall produce,
> And evil turn to good; more wonderful
> Than that which by creation first brought forth
> Light out of darkness! full of doubt I stand,
> Whether I should repent me now of sin
> By mee done and occasion'd, or rejoice
> Much more, that much more good thereof shall spring,
> To God more glory, more good to Men
> From God, and over wrath grace shall abound.[4]

LIKE MOST twenty-first-century American poets, I swim in the warm and shallow waters of the personal. My poems are, for the most part, very interested in me. They like what I like; they fear what I fear—"to themselves appropriating / The Spirit of God." The unpleasant notion that writing poems may require me to compromise my private tastes and idiosyncrasies strikes me cold, for contemporary poets tend to be idealists only insofar as our ideals mirror our personal predilections. Unlike social workers or schoolteachers or nurses, we don't find ourselves treading the line between system and individual; we don't find ourselves constrained by the modest, incremental, daily costs of failing to save another person's life.

> O by what Name, for thou above all these,
> Above mankind, or aught than mankind higher,
> Surpassest far my naming, how may I
> Adore thee, Author of this Universe.[5]

This is the question that new-made Adam proffers to God; and despite its distracting obsequiousness, it's a question that I believe Milton asked both of himself and of God. Nor is it a coincidence that, throughout the poem, he refers to God (and sometimes Satan) as "author." Writing the universe, writing the poem, writing sin: in all cases the author imagines and creates under conditions of intense and influential responsibility. Adam's question, then, does more than admire or beg for intercession; it is a request for precise information. What's your name, maker, and "how may I / Adore thee"? Man's first task in paradise is to verify his proper responsibilities.

And Milton's proper responsibilities? Before hitting his polemical stride in *Paradise Lost*, he was shyer about them. At twenty-nine he was still embarrassed to mention his plans, even to his closest friend: "Listen, Diodati, but in secret, lest I blush; and let me talk to you grandiloquently for a while. You ask what I am thinking of? So help me God, an immortality of fame. What am I doing? Growing my wings and practicing flight. But my Pegasus still raises himself on very tender wings."[6]

Though a blushing Milton is a rare endearing image, and I like to picture him as a sharp-elbowed youth gnawing his lower lip and turning blotchy, this man who set his sights so coolly on "an

immortality of fame" couldn't have actually wasted much time on
the pangs of embarrassment. What the rest of us might call dreams
seem in his case more like a job description.

> Hast thou not made me here thy substitute,
> And these inferiors far beneath me set?
> Among unequals what society
> Can sort, what harmony or true delight?[7]

It's a tricky business, showing other people how to fix themselves;
and according to the patriarchal rulebook, one can't really accomplish
that job by standing companionably alongside the misguided like a
pal. Ergo pulpits and big glossy desks and mysterious unreadable
hospital charts. "Oft-times nothing profits more / Than self-esteem"
may sound like a gentle, liberal approach to self-help, but in *Paradise
Lost* it's a useful instrument of subjugation, "grounded on just and
right / Well manag'd." As God tells Adam, "of that skill the more
thou know'st, / The more [Eve] will acknowledge thee her Head."
In other words, contentment derives from both obedience to the
boss and strict management of inferiors, whether beast or wife.[8]

Being the wife, I naturally find this stuff dispiriting. Over the
course of my *Paradise Lost* odyssey, I've tried hard to grapple with
Milton the poet and the man as opposed to Milton the shrill
woman-negating pedagogue. But after a certain point it's no longer
possible to avoid that shadow. He is, after all, the bozo who once
declared, "When God originally gave man a wife he intended her
to be his help, solace and delight. So if, as often happens, she is
found to be a source of grief, shame, deception, ruin and calamity
instead, why should we think it displeasing to God if we divorce
her?" Why indeed?[9]

The problem with inspirational argument is that it tends to
inspire only a select audience. Adam's apparently rational conception of happiness—"conversation with his like to help, / Or solace

his defects"—seems also to be Milton's; yet Milton's conception of happiness was clearly not his first wife's, igniter of his bitter thoughts on divorce, nor her daughters', to whom he willed an unpaid debt ("they haveing ben very undutiful to me"). I might speculate on the discontent that drove his seventeen-year-old wife back to her father's house after roughly two months of marriage. I might speculate on the discontent that drove her to return to her crabby husband three years later and bear him four children before dying in childbirth. But none of my speculations will lead me to believe that reading *Paradise Lost*'s recommendations for wife management (as in "be not diffident / Of Wisdom . . . / By attributing overmuch to things / Less excellent") would have increased her felicity.[10]

Things less excellent. Sometimes I feel my entire world is built on things less excellent: folding shabby towels and slicing crooked loaves, dramatically intoning my son's spelling list, picking burrs out of the dog's ears in front of a sputtering woodstove. They're all stupid and boring and contribute to my ravenous discontent on those days when I'm boxed in by my inability to earn any money or to ever achieve, "so help me God, an immortality of fame." It's one thing for women's inspirational literature—*Cranford*, for instance, or *Mrs. Dalloway*—to promote these things less excellent as the essence of a rich and living spirit. I'm convinced they *are* worthwhile when I read those novels. I believe in them with all my heart during the last warm days of September, when the harvest is king and I'm scalding and peeling and canning bushel after bushel of tomatoes, contented to be a housewife, proud as a poet of my twenty scarlet quarts and my acid-pickled hands. But in *Paradise Lost* Milton relegates such valuables to women as he might relegate scratching to chickens or swimming to eels: "inferior, infinite descents." And when I read the poem I am aware, constantly, that a woman's distress about the shifting and ambiguous meanings of happiness counts for nothing.[11]

When Eve learns, after the fall, that she and Adam must leave Eden, she weeps—for her failure in obedience, yes, but also for the loss of her things less excellent: those well-loved details of her daily life.

> O unexpected stroke, worse than of Death!
> Must I leave thee Paradise? thus leave
> Thee Native Soil, these happy Walks and Shades,
> Fit haunt of Gods? where I had hope to spend,
> Quiet though sad, the respite of that day
> That must be mortal to us both. O flow'rs,
> That never will in other Climate grow,
> My early visitation, and my last
> At Ev'n, which I bred up with tender hand
> From the first op'ning bud, and gave ye Names,
> Who now shall rear ye to the Sun, or rank
> Your Tribes, and water from th' ambrosial Fount?
> Thee lastly nuptial Bower, by mee adorn'd
> With what to sight or smell was sweet; from thee
> How shall I part, and whither wander down
> Into a lower World, to this obscure
> And wild, how shall we breathe other Air
> Less pure, accustom'd to immortal Fruits?

But the angel Michael rebukes her tears:

> Lament not *Eve*, but patiently resign
> What justly thou hast lost; nor set thy heart,
> Thus over-fond, on that which is not thine;
> Thy going is not lonely, with thee goes
> Thy Husband, him to follow thou art bound;
> Where he abides, think there thy native soil.[12]

Without question I love Tom more than I love living in Harmony. "Where he abides," I want to be—even, I suppose, if that means a condo association in the Chicago suburbs (though he'd never have such a bad idea). But he is not the sum total of my native soil. For all of us, men and women alike, our native soil is the layered history of our lives: the books we've studied, the rows we've tilled, our "happy Walks and Shades," our "sorrow and heart's distress." Eve's life may be wrapped up in Adam's, but it's also wrapped up in her private labors and affections. So why is she scorned for lamenting the loss of the flowers she "bred up with tender hand"? I find it hard to believe that Milton would have kept his temper if Michael had quick-marched him out of Eden with *Paradise Lost* left half-written on the table.

But then that's the story of death, isn't it? And while Milton didn't much lament the loss of his first wife, he did weep for his second—his "late espousèd saint"—also dead in childbirth. The sonnet he wrote in mourning encapsulates his peculiar ability to undercut pomposity with tenderness, nearly by accident, it seems, since the poem treads tendentiously through her mythological perfections, "washed from spot of childbed taint," until the final lines:

> Love, sweetness, goodness, in her person shined
> So clear as in no face with more delight,
> But O as to embrace me she inclined,
> I waked, she fled, and day brought back my night.[13]

It's a sad and lovely ending, and I pity the lonely man who wrote it, bereft again, left to carry the burden of his children and himself, without, in Adam's words, "those graceful acts / those thousand decencies that daily flow / From all her words and actions." Yet when I compare "On His Dead Wife" to the opening lines of his contemporary Anne Bradstreet's most famous poem, I realize that Milton never did understand what it means to capture the bright essence of human contentment. In "To My Dear and Loving Husband" Bradstreet begins:

> If ever two were one, then surely we.
> If ever man were loved by wife, then thee;
> If ever wife was happy in a man,
> Compare with me, ye women, if you can.[14]

Technically, intellectually, cosmically, Milton, "the Oracle of God," takes home the master-poet prize. But Bradstreet's poem *is* happiness . . . an instant of contentment, embraced. No doubt, within half an hour her husband was annoying her again—dropping butter down the front of his linen shirt, slamming a door during a baby's nap. Yet she manages, in her simple square lines, to make me know she was happy, and to be happy myself.[15]

But happiness in *Paradise Lost?* Even in the throes of sexual joy, Adam points out the shortcomings of his new wife, who may be "in outward show / Elaborate" but is "of inward less exact," his "inferior, in the mind / And inward Faculties / . . . and less expressing / The character of Dominion giv'n / O'er other Creatures." If my husband talked about me like that, he certainly would not increase my happiness—or his. So did Milton learn a lesson from his quarrels with his first wife and manage to abstain from such blather with the second and third? Were the later wives able to nurture their happiness in a "native soil" composed of something other than their pontificating husband—perhaps the labor of their bodies, perhaps their own secret visions and perceptions? Or did they hear, in his windbag instructions, a more complicated story: a fear of solitude or loss or weakness? In *Brief Lives,* John Aubrey writes that Milton "would be cheerful even in his gout-fits and sing." Did his wives hear, in "his gout-fits," a clumsy, gallant pride?[16]

> though all the Stars
> Thou knew'st by name, and all th' ethereal Powers,
> All secrets of the deep, all Nature's works,
> Or works of God in Heav'n, Air, Earth, or Sea,

> And all the riches of this World enjoy'dst,
> And all the rule, one Empire; only add
> Deeds to thy knowledge answerable, add Faith,
> Add Virtue, Patience, Temperance, add Love,
> By name to come call'd Charity, the soul
> Of all the rest: then wilt thou not be loath
> To leave this Paradise, but shalt possess
> A paradise within thee, happier far.[17]

As retort to his complaints about Eve, Adam receives a few brisk instructions from Raphael about the niceties of love and married happiness:

> Love refines
> The thoughts, and heart enlarges, hath his seat
> In Reason, and is judicious, is the scale
> By which to heav'nly Love thou may'st ascend.

Yet as Raphael concedes, "thy mate . . . sees when thou art seen least wise." There is a certain happiness in recognizing one's capacity to love what is difficult to love: the three-legged hamster, the taciturn husband, the obnoxious child, the loneliness of snow, the dull perplexities of grammar, "the petty disputations of sour old men." Dear Milton. Maybe someone did miss you when you were gone.[18]

11
Killing Ruthie

Forth issuing on a Summer's Morn to breathe
Among the pleasant Villages and Farms
Adjoin'd, from each thing met conceives delight,
The smell of Grain, or tedded Grass, or Kine,
Or Dairy, each rural sight, each rural sound.

I ASKED MY FRIEND STEVE to shoot my goat.

Steve is what his wife calls "a born-again redneck." His parents are genteel, well-educated, violin-playing Quakers, but Steve decided not to graduate from high school. He preferred to educate himself, and now he knows what ants taste like ("fruity") and how to turn raccoons into a couch blanket. Steve is a man who can efficiently pull a trigger but won't scorn you if you cry. Among men who handle guns, this is not a common trait.

He said he could shoot my goat on Sunday morning, though he wasn't in the mood to get tied up with butchering.

I said I would dig a hole.

My goat's name was Ruthie, a black and white American Alpine, eleven years old. She'd had breathing problems, an off-and-on panting snuffle, for six months or so. I called the vet, who said parasites might be migrating into her lungs. After I dosed her with wormer, she seemed maybe a little better, maybe the same. She ate as much as a Clydesdale, but she was thin and her hair was sloughing off in handfuls.

Eventually the vet dropped by and listened to the snuffle. Ruthie gobbled grain and snorted and bulged her eyes zestfully. The vet, muscle-bound and taciturn, said eleven was fairly old for a goat. She said maybe it was allergies but most likely not. The word *cancer* was not uttered. Sunlight seeped through the barn's grimy windows, flickered among the hanks of ancient spider webs dangling from the rafters. The barn smelled of dust and last summer's hay, vaguely of manure, more richly of repose, as a room in a house can smell of sleep.

Ruth licked the last grain flecks out of her plastic dish, tossed it upside down and rapped it with a black hoof, then snuffled and lurched onto my son's bare foot. He yelped. "Wear boots," I said to him.

"Prepare yourself," said the vet.

THE MOMENTS BEFORE a catastrophe seem always, in retrospect, to be a fraught and melancholy prelude, a "Proem tun'd." But when a participant has contrived that portending disaster, the crowd's interactive ignorance may assume a formal and symbolic innocence, a point that Wisława Szymborska elucidates in her poem "The Terrorist, He's Watching." Her terrorist's omniscient eye stylizes the clueless actions of the bystanders, flattening them into a dancelike pattern that incorporates as well the man's own murderous intent.[1]

In *Paradise Lost*, the relationship between Satan and Eve has a similar stylized inevitability; and Satan, that elegant Nabokovian villain, expends considerable thought on the trembling pleasures and pangs of anticipated evil. Connoisseur that he is, he enjoys skating along the fragile icy crust between right and wrong; he looks forward to soiling Eve's perfection even as he admires its beauty. He goes so far as to allow "her graceful Innocence" to disarm him—temporarily:

> her every Air
> Of gesture or least action overaw'd
> His Malice, and with rapine sweet bereav'd
> His fierceness of the fierce intent it brought:
> That space the Evil one abstracted stood
> From his own evil, and for the time remain'd
> Stupidly good, or enmity disarm'd,
> Of guile, of hate, of envy, of revenge.[2]

When one chooses to murder an animal, there is, in the hours and minutes preceding the act, a similar hiatus. On Sunday morning I was "stupidly good," weighed down by my bad intentions as well as by a calm patient kindness, both of them nailed to my conscience like Soviet posters on a plank fence. I considered the permutations of my wickedness and admired the shiny barrel of its gun. My conscience commented conversationally, "If you weren't going to Brooklyn in a week, you wouldn't dream of executing this goat today. It's a matter of convenience."

I replied, "No doubt she's suffering terrible pain," and sighed.

The artistic imagination—in this case, the simultaneous ability to experience grief and aesthetically reconfigure it—is both a marvelous distraction and a guilty torment, and one of Milton's great triumphs in his delineation of Satan is the way in which he guides the reader through the Fiend's coiling artistic intellect. In the final moments before Satan, in serpent guise, accosts Eve and cajoles her into betraying God's word and eating from the Tree of

Knowledge, he meditates on his mind's vivid powers, the way in which his intellect detaches itself from the event and examines it clinically, aesthetically, with a ruthless clarity.

> Thoughts, whither have ye led me, with what sweet
> Compulsion thus transported to forget
> What hither brought us, hate, not love, nor hope
> Of Paradise for Hell, hope here to taste
> Of pleasure, but all pleasure to destroy,
> Save what is in destroying, other joy
> To me is lost.[3]

He's not entirely happy with himself, certainly. Satan would prefer to be a single-minded villain, as God, "the Father infinite," is a single-minded king. Yet he recognizes his double bind: humans, "though of terrestrial mould," are, like gods, still exempt from suffering. The Fiend, a fallen angel, is not, "so much hath Hell debas'd, and pain / Infeebl'd me, to what I was in Heav'n." Evil he is, yet pitiable; for guile, "under show of Love well feign'd," distracts the deceiver from self-excoriation, doubt, and guilt. He tells Eve:

> The Gods are first, and that advantage use
> On our belief, that all from them proceeds;
> I question it, for this fair Earth I see,
> Warm'd by the Sun, producing every kind,
> Them nothing: If they all things, who enclos'd
> Knowledge of Good and Evil in this Tree,
> That so eats thereof, forthwith attains
> Wisdom without their leave? and wherein lies
> Th' offense, that Man should thus attain to know?
> What can your knowledge hurt him, or this Tree
> Impart against his will if all be his?
> Or is it envy, and can envy dwell
> In heav'nly breasts?[4]

His questions are both honest and false. He may be asking them in order to delude his listener; but he's also a sufferer, and one who has no answers.

BEFORE YOU KILL A GOAT, you have to dig a grave, preferably close to the murder site so you don't have to drag the body too far. A full-grown dairy goat weighs as much as an average woman—Eve, for instance—but the grave can't be human-shaped. You need a square hole to accommodate those four skinny legs.

I fetched a spade from the chicken house and began scratching at likely patches of earth near the barn. Hand-digging a goat-sized hole in a New England forest is not a simple matter, and my choice of location was limited. In addition to harboring a tangle of spruce and pine roots, many as thick as my arm, the soil on the boundary of our clearing is dense with rock: wedges of slate, granite boulders, chunks of dirty luminous quartz. It's nigh on impossible to imagine a farmer plowing this ground, though once he did. He would weep to see it now, my rocky wilderness. Like scrub poplar and wild raspberries, stone reclaims.

The morning threatened storm. A silver fog hung over the trellised pea vines, heavy with rainwater and swelling fruit. The vines sagged like wet towels into the garden paths. On her side of the barnyard fence Ruthie snorted and coughed, lifting a foot now and then to shake off a fly as I scratched an estimated tomb pattern on the weedy verge. She wasn't exactly watching me. More, her presence radiated that combined interest-disinterest of familiars long penned up in the same garden. Affection is not the point in such cases. Trust stems from custom: you are always here; I am always here.

It is precisely this humdrum contiguity, this ordinary elbow rubbing, that Satan manipulates in his initial encounter with Eve.

If he had appeared in all his Fiendish glory, brandishing his fiery trident, she would never have succumbed to his wiles. Instead,

> With tract oblique
> At first, as one who sought access, but fear'd
> To interrupt, side-long, he works his way.
> As when a Ship by skilful Steersman wrought
> Nigh River's mouth or Foreland, where the Wind
> Veers oft, as oft so steers, and shifts her Sail;
> So varied hee, and of his tortuous Train
> Curl'd many a wanton wreath in sight of *Eve*,
> To lure her Eye; shee busied heard the sound
> Of rustling Leaves, but minded not, as us'd
> To such disport before her through the Field,
> From every Beast, more duteous at her call,
> Than at Circean call the Herd disguis'd.[5]

Milton's allusion to Circe and her magicked swine is curious. Proper sex roles are always important matters to this poet, so aligning the tricksters Circe and Satan against Odysseus' enchanted seamen and "amaz'd unwary" Eve is a notable inversion. Yet even as he toys with this mythological parallel, he resists the comparison: it's Eve whose "Circean call" controls "the Herd disguis'd"; it's the "duteous" Fiend who "disport[s] before her through the Field." Guile and innocence flow and shift and mutate as the characters play out their fateful game.

> His gentle dumb expression turn'd at length
> The Eye of *Eve* to mark his play; he glad
> Of her attention gain'd, with Serpent Tongue
> Organic, or impulse of vocal Air,
> His fraudulent temptation thus began.[6]

Satan chooses, of course, that depressingly effective device, feminine temptation. Accustomed as she is to being Adam's obedient, not-too-bright helpmeet, Eve is encouraged to reimagine herself as "sole Wonder," "Beauty's heav'nly Ray," "Sovran of Creatures, universal Dame." "So gloz'd the Tempter," praising her "Celestial Beauty," declaring her "a Goddess among Gods" who should be "ador'd and serv'd / By Angels numberless." Yet his flattery delves deeper than mere "ravishment": he seizes her attention, and her trust, by speaking her language. Amazed, she asks the serpent:

> What may this mean? Language of Man pronounc't
> By Tongue of Brute, and human sense exprest?
> The first at least of these I thought deni'd
> To Beasts, whom God on thir Creation-Day
> Created mute to all articulate sound.[7]

Here, indeed, is the crux of our power over the lives of animals. Would I have planned Ruthie's killing if she had spoken the "Language of Man" through the barnyard gate? Would she have lived her entire life behind that fence? Would I have sold her children, arranged her fornications, and exhibited her publicly at county fairs? Where does slavery end and husbandry begin? Despite his malice, the serpent "with human voice endu'd" is a clarion for all "beasts that graze / The trodden Herb." He forces me, as he forces Eve, to reconsider "the rest / Of brutal kind, that daily are in sight."[8]

The narrative of temptation drives Book IX of *Paradise Lost*; and because Milton is anxious to lure Eve to the Tree of Knowledge, he doesn't linger over the astonishments of a talking serpent. The humans—both poet and character—instantly habituate themselves to snaky conversation. But I find myself revisiting again and again this moment of revelation, "redoubl[ing] this miracle," the instant when a silent creature "cam'st . . . speakable of mute" and "human sense exprest." What if God had seen fit, from the beginning, to allow humans and beasts to speak freely to one another? What if I needed to *ask* Ruthie if she were ready to die?[9]

I DREAMED LAST NIGHT that my bathroom was full of hungry cats and kittens, perhaps twenty or thirty of them mewling and scratching and wailing. Gnawed toothbrushes and soap were overturned on the floor; towels were slashed and filthy. The room stank of cat urine, and the floor was littered with straw. I embraced an armful of cats; I tried to carry them away, but they slipped from my grasp, slick as eels: yet I knew they were desperate, desperate for my care.

The anxieties of animal rearing are legion. So much can go wrong. What about an enormous buck kid jammed in his mother's birth canal, his tongue squeezed in agony between his blunt teeth, as his mother screams and screams and screams? A shotgun to the head must surely be a release. These animals, "of abject thoughts and low," who "aught but food discern . . . / Or Sex," impel us, as caretakers, to manufacture the appropriate final solution. Or that is what the farmer schools herself to believe. "For in thir looks," as Eve affirms, "Much reason, and in thir actions oft appears." And their looks, though sometimes frightened, frenzied, morose, or belligerent, do not accuse us of treachery.[10]

Ruthie's body was shrinking, withering. Her yellow eyes glittered. Her droppings were loose, sour, like a sick child's. She snorted and panted and left foamy traces of mucus in the water buckets. I believed that she was incurably ill, suffering at least constant discomfort if not actual pain, and was too weak to endure another Maine winter. She was not able to tell me otherwise. And I was able to arrange her death because I knew she would succumb to temptation.

> On a day roving the field, I chanc'd
> A goodly Tree far distant to behold
> Loaden with fruit of fairest colors mixt,
> Ruddy and Gold: I drew nearer to gaze;
> When from the boughs a savory odor blown,

Grateful to appetite, more pleas'd my sense
Than smell of sweetest Fennel, or the Teats
Of Ewe or Goat dropping with Milk at Ev'n,
Unsuckt of Lamb or Kid, that tend thir play.[11]

Greed "urg'd . . . so keen" is not exclusively a human trait. The instinct of all living things is to consume as much as we can get, as fast as we can get it. The serpent tells Eve, "To satisfy the sharp desire I had / Of tasting those fair Apples, I resolv'd / Not to defer."

About the mossy Trunk I wound me soon,
For high from ground the branches would require
Thy utmost reach or *Adam's*: Round the Tree
All other Beasts that saw, with like desire
Longing and envying stood, but could not reach.[12]

The tale is false, of course. The incident Satan describes was concocted as trickery. But Eve falls for the story: they *seem* real to her, "that alluring fruit," the animals "with like desire." For instinctively we recognize the truth of seduction and desire; and if that recognition is, perhaps, our deepest bond with the animal world, it is also, as Satan proves, our locus of dominion.

Amid the Tree now got, where plenty hung
Tempting so nigh, to pluck and eat my fill
I spar'd not, for such pleasure till that hour
At Feed or Fountain never had I found.[13]

I lured Ruthie to her death with a bowlful of grain. As soon as she heard the clank of the grain-bin lid, she rushed to the gate, neck stretched, eyes popping. Eagerly, she watched me scoop the sticky mix of pellets and oats and cracked corn into her green plastic dish. Eagerly, she stamped her feet at the door—impatient, single-minded. I opened the gate, held the dish high, out of her grasping, wriggling reach, and with the other hand snapped a leash to her shabby collar.

> But say, where grows the Tree, from hence how far?
> For many are the Trees of God that grow
> In Paradise, and various, yet unknown
> To us, in such abundance lies our choice.[14]

We tied her, Steve and I, to a steel barrel beside a tree, a common spruce tree, one of a hundred, a thousand, spruce trees spearing our grey northern sky; these ordinary trees whose roots writhe beneath our shallow acid soil; those tough, twisted roots I had so lately been hacking with my sexton's spade.

> Empress, the way is ready, and not long,
> Beyond a row of Myrtles, on a Flat,
> Fast by a Fountain, one small Thicket past
> Of blowing Myrrh and Balm; if thou accept
> My conduct, I can bring thee thither soon.[15]

Ruthie yanked and tugged at the short leash in gluttonous desperation. Fog clung, like comfort, to the lilacs, the dripping chokecherries, the serrated weeds along the forest edge. I laid the dish of grain on the ground before the goat, and she ducked her head into the bowl, gobbling fast, noisily, without thought or thanks.

> Intent now wholly on her taste, naught else
> Regarded, such delight till then, as seem'd,
> In Fruit she never tasted, whether true
> Or fancied so, through expectation high
> Of knowledge, nor was God-head from her thought.
> Greedily she ingorg'd without restraint,
> And knew not eating Death.[16]

I left her with Steve and walked away, into my garden.

12

Dust

Curs'd is the ground for thy sake, thou in sorrow
Shalt eat thereof all the days of thy Life;
Thorns also and Thistles it shall bring thee forth
Unbid, and thou shalt eat th' Herb of the Field,
In the sweat of thy Face shalt thou eat Bread,
Till thou return unto the ground, for thou
Out of the ground wast taken, know thy Birth,
For dust thou art, and shalt to dust return.

Over the course of this self-imposed reading assignment, I've spent a good deal of time not liking Adam and Eve, or their tame forest, or their smarmy heavenly protectors. I've complained about them and ridiculed them and heaved gusty sighs of despair. In large part, I haven't *wanted* to care about them. I've wanted to ignore them, refigure them, tart them up. I've wanted to tear them out of the coloring book and lose them under the couch cushions. I have indeed wanted to discover and argue with and possess Milton and all of his crazy greatness. But I haven't wanted to love this stilted, static pair.

Nonetheless I do love them, though in this case the connotations of *love* are imprecise and difficult to negotiate. I can't love them like parents or objects of desire, despite Milton's relentless encouragement. Nor can I disguise myself in their personae, as I might with Huck Finn or Elizabeth Bennet. Nor can I exactly admire them as fractured reflections of a familiar world, as I do Chaucer's pilgrims to Canterbury or Dickens's Aged Parent.

My feelings about Adam and Eve bear more resemblance to the love I once felt for my large and shabby collection of dolls and stuffed bears: a general helpless, anxious, immersed affection blent with indifference; a superstitious physical attachment; a periodic ferocious, godlike control over these button-eyed companions, whom I riotously embraced for a season and then forgot for the rest of my life. Like battered rag dolls, Eve and Adam are emblems of the grief and ruthlessness of time.

Of course, in truth I have no control over these characters. Come innocence or sorrow, they wend their augured way, "hand in hand with wand'ring steps and slow." The inevitability of myth is a well-oiled yet melancholy trap. Like the life stories of the noble dead, a myth is both stately and inexorable. Again, and once more again, Virginia Woolf wades into the river with her sweater pockets full of stones, John Keats sails hopelessly to Italy, Pandora unlocks her forbidden casket.[1]

And so Adam and Eve's lost paradise is also my lost paradise, not because I ever glimpsed it or even had faith in its existence but because the tale of their loss dwells with me, as legends do, in the shadowy margins between knowledge and invention. A prodigious experiment, this devouring of myth, a willing obedience to the delights and tragedies of belief. If story helps us rationalize mystery, it also absorbs us into sensibility's bosky underworld. We become the sadness we know.

This is why myth, for all its implausibility, seems so much like lived experience. There is nothing real about Prometheus chained to the rock or Orpheus looking back for Eurydice. They could not have existed. And yet they have always existed, even in Harmony, Maine, in the autumn of the year, where webworm nests swing triumphantly in the chokecherries and my nine-year-old son tosses long, wobbly football spirals, his trajectory a slow-motion wiggle into the weeds.

> O Parent, these are thy magnific deeds,
> Thy Trophies, which thou view'st as not thine own,
> Thou art thir Author and prime Architect.[2]

This is the key to myth—that I stand inside and outside it simultaneously. I taste Eve's apple and I believe the serpent's words with all my laden heart, which "by a secret harmony / Still moves with thine," my "Author and prime Architect," as my son's football blunders into the weeds, as a hen squawks irritably, as Sin and Death await Satan at the foot of the "portentous Bridge" they have built over the gates of Hell.

For it is Sin who speaks so confidingly of her "Author"; it is she whose "wondrous Pontifrice" links her "in connexion sweet" to her father and lover, her writer and reader. Our sins are the story that lives forever.[3]

I sit at my desk, listening to a warm September wind groan through the window casings, to a jay argue with a squirrel, and I wonder what to do with myself now that paradise has forsaken me. The story ends. Slowly Milton stands, easing his stiff knees. He clears his throat, blinks his cloudy eyes. A small clatter; the amanuensis has dropped her pen. A dab of ink pools on the margin of the page. It swells; it dissolves into a branching stain.

Although the creation of paradise was predicated on innocence, the creation of *Paradise Lost* required sin. Without sin, Milton would have had no tale to tell, no morals to render, no curiosities to sate, no perfections to invent. "Such fatal consequence unites us three," story, sin, and paradise. As Satan tells his demons,

> Long were to tell
> What I have done, what suffer'd, with what pain
> Voyag'd th' unreal, vast, unbounded deep
> Of horrible confusion.[4]

But this is the tale we want to hear, and to tell, again and again and again.

I sit at my desk. It's noon, a warm late September day—too warm, really, for Maine in the autumn. The heat seems unreal, ominous. Out of sight, a squirrel dashes back and forth across the roof. His steps sound heavy and hoofed, like a scurrying antelope's, and he's surely up to no good.

> Thence how I found
> The new created World, which fame in Heav'n
> Long had foretold, a Fabric wonderful
> Of absolute perfection.[5]

Before I stumbled into becoming a poet, I believed that poetry was a great calling, perhaps the highest: rich, noble, austere. I believed that poets were the mouthpiece of our collective grace. "But dust thou art, and shalt to dust return"; and once I admitted myself into their august company, I found myself choking for breath in a dirty cloud of poetic ire and doubt, not to mention clumsiness and arrogance and plain bad intentions. My late acquaintance with Milton has done nothing to soften that shock. Despite his youthful proclamation, "it is my lot to have been born a poet," he wielded his powers like a broadsword, to spear and batter and mislead; and he excoriated those less proficient with their weapons—calling a rival pamphleteer a "tormentor of semicolons . . . as good at dismembering and slitting sentences, as his grave Fathers the Prelates have been at stigmatizing & slitting noses"; going so far as to libel a bishop with a neat litany of his very own faults: "[He] never knew the soyle, never handl'd a Dibble or Spade to set the least potherbe that grew there, much lesse had endur'd an houres sweat or chilnesse, and yet challenges as his right the binding or unbinding of every flower, the clipping of every bush, the weeding and worming of every bed." Remind me: which bossy, controlling person are we talking about here?[6]

Yet as Satan asks, who "a World . . . would not purchase with a bruise, / Or much more grievous pain?" Doesn't every desperate, earnest poet strive to live by this query? . . . not to mention every ambitious minor league knuckleball pitcher; every starving, honor-wrenched arctic explorer; every jumpy, wiry, hair-on-end kindergarten teacher? They're all idealists, chasing perfection of one sort or another. Yet in Milton's ruthless vision, the chase is futile. We may "to Paradise first [be] tending," yet we're all seduced; we all fail; we all "behold *Satan* in likeness of an Angel bright."[7]

In a handful of stunningly beautiful lines, perhaps the greatest poetry of the poem, Adam mourns his bereavement:

> How shall I behold the face
> Henceforth of God or Angel, erst with joy
> And rapture so oft beheld? those heav'nly shapes
> Will dazzle now this earthly, with thir blaze
> Insufferably bright. O might I here
> In solitude live savage, in some glade
> Obscur'd, where highest Woods impenetrable
> To Star or Sun-light, spread thir umbrage broad,
> And brown as Evening: Cover me, ye Pines,
> Ye Cedars, with innumerable boughs
> Hide me, where I may never see them more.[8]

By means of these vivid, bewildering lines, Adam cries out the exquisite measured anguish, the ancient, austere grief of his people; he speaks in the plangent tongue of the prophet, the hero, the poet. Yet he mourns not so much his loss of personal innocence as his newfound inability to contemplate heavenly perfection. We can look at Satan as freely as we like, but we can no longer meet the eyes of God.

I came to the woods to make a new life. I came to the woods to hide my shame. Milton takes pains to announce to posterity that I've done both simultaneously and that I'm a fool to think either attempt will do me any good. But he gives me the same small break that he gave to the unfortunate bishop: he writes about my stupid illusions in language that exactly depicts his own stupid illusions. And he does this not by maneuvering my angle of pity as a way of taking the heat off himself. He does it by lifting his blind gaze and staring straight into Satan's eyes.

> Ye have th' account
> Of my performance: What remains, ye Gods,
> But up and enter now into full bliss?[9]

This is Satan's triumphant query to his demons, and it might well have been Milton's question to himself as he staggered toward the end of the ordeal that is *Paradise Lost*.

> So having said, a while he stood, expecting
> Thir universal shout and high applause
> To fill his ear, when contrary he hears
> On all sides, from innumerable tongues
> A dismal universal hiss, the sound
> Of public scorn; he wonder'd, but not long
> Had leisure, wond'ring at himself now more;
> His Visage drawn he felt to sharp and spare,
> His Arms clung to his Ribs, his Legs entwining
> Each other, till supplanted down he fell
> A monstrous Serpent on his Belly prone,
> Reluctant, but in vain: a greater power
> Now rul'd him, punish't in the shape he sinn'd.[10]

Perhaps Milton, too, was "punish't in the shape he sinn'd." His vision was his pride, his gift, and his downfall. The "dismal universal hiss, the sound of public scorn," sibilates even yet, these years and decades and centuries since his death. He is forever with us, great historian of a great, ridiculous, beautiful, tragic myth of our species; yet we've forgotten him also—misplaced him, fawned over him, derided him, flayed him into pertinent bits.

Milton, c'est moi, is a glib reduction, signature flourish of an individualistic Romantic tradition he would have abhorred. But though myth may be durable, it is not immutable. With all due respect, J.M., you're not in charge of every story. "In some glade / Obscur'd, where highest Woods impenetrable / To Star or Sun-light, spread thir umbrage broad," there's a woman sitting alone at her desk. She's not sweeping a floor or instructing her sons or collecting eggs or hauling firewood or embracing her husband. She does all of those things every day, and she'll get back to them eventually, but right now she doesn't have time for them.

She's busy reading your book.

Afterword

Chief of organic numbers!
Old Scholar of the Spheres!
Thy spirit never slumbers,
But rolls about our ears
For ever and for ever!

—JOHN KEATS,
"On Seeing a Lock of Milton's
Hair" (1818)

IN EARLY DECEMBER 2007 I finished copying out the final lines of *Paradise Lost*. Accomplishing the job had occupied me sporadically but steadily for more than two years. Some weeks I copied out page after page. Some weeks I managed only a few lines. Some hours my fingers chased each other fluidly over the keyboard like Rogers and Astaire sparkling in easy tandem across a spotlit stage. Some hours I mangled every word, stuttering through typos and flawed punctuation, misunderstood verbs and unanticipated line breaks—an epic chore narrowed to "backspace and try again, backspace and try again."

Copying was a hard job, and not just because typing is dull and Milton is a mountain. Living with myself as copyist was equivalently hard. When I undertook the task, I thought of myself as a poet, not a memoirist. But I was anxious about my worth as a poet: I needed to do something important, something improving. Transcribing Milton's masterpiece seemed to be a quick solution and a weighty preoccupation, yet I couldn't define why it might be improving or important. Even though I saw the job as special, even glamorous, I couldn't take myself seriously. That I may have been the only person on the planet who imagined copying out all of *Paradise Lost* to be glamorous increased both my absurdity and my conceit. And once I began to write about the project, my sense of inadequacy grew. As hard as I pressed myself intellectually, I could not, in the end, truly understand *Paradise Lost*. The poem was too large for me.

My friend Meg reminded me not to let self-deprecation get in the way of discovery. Why shouldn't I be proud of grappling with Milton on my own territory? Why shouldn't I be thrilled by the workings of my own mind? She had a point. But unfortunately, humility and painful embarrassment seem to be part of the bride-price of wrestling with Milton. Even Keats ruefully said as much. The young poet desperately admired Milton; yet despite "feeling grateful as I do to have got into a state of mind to relish [his philosophy] properly," he admitted he could not comprehend the master's greatness. For Keats, as for most of the rest of us regular human beings, "nothing ever becomes real till it is experienced—Even a Proverb is no proverb to you till your Life has illustrated it."[1]

But now that I've resumed a Milton-free life, I begin to see that he lingers, he teaches, he guides—not as a philosopher, to be sure, but as a poet. I may not have absorbed the doctrinal and intellectual underpinnings of *Paradise Lost*, but the structural edifice of the poem became real to me because I experienced it word by word, line by line, day after day after day. And what a miracle his storytelling is—a flexible, digressive arc marked by bursts of intensity and withdrawal, of lyric and frame. How could writers like Virginia Woolf and Henry Green have existed without the buttress of this stodgy old Puritan and his magical fusion of story and sensibility? Yet even though his narrative style predicts the innovations of prose modernism, he remains a poet, a bard, invoking his dense and "advent'rous song." Keats wrote poems because Milton's meter rang and echoed in his ears. And now it is ringing in mine.

> How soon hath thy prediction, Seer blest,
> Measur'd this transient World, the Race of time,
> Till time stand fixt.[2]

Experiencing the poem, following its every step down every page, has given me such hope for my own work. It has shown me that the nobility of poetry lies in its artisan commitment to language as a venture into wonder. Poets *think* their way into mystery: deliberation builds on accident; accident builds on deliberation. "What in me is dark / Illumine, what is low raise and support." In *Paradise Lost*, Milton writes his vision of the cosmos. But he also invites me to write my own.[3]

Notes

Opening epigraph quoted in Barbara K. Lewalski, *The Life of John Milton* (Oxford: Blackwell, 2000), 44. The frontispiece, Jonathan Fisher's *Forlorn Maiden*, is reproduced from an original woodcut in the Farnsworth Art Museum. All other interior illustrations are from Jonathan Fisher's *Scripture Animals, or Natural History of the Living Creatures Named in the Bible Written Especially for Youth Illustrated with Cuts* (Portland, Maine: Hyde, 1834).

Chapter 1: Chores

Epigraph: John Milton, *Paradise Lost* (1667), ed. Merritt Y. Hughes (Indianapolis: Odyssey, 1962), book 7, lines 210–15, hereafter cited as 7:210–15. Unless otherwise noted, all further quotations are from *Paradise Lost*.

1. 1:242–45.
2. 4:533–35.
3. 4:299.
4. 11:829–38.
5. 5:331, 347.
6. 3:68.
7. 2:481–82.

Chapter 2: Stumbling into Harmony

Epigraph: 4:246–47.
1. 2:165–68.
2. Thomas Hardy, "The Dorsetshire Laborer," *Longman's* (July 1883), quoted in John Fowles, "Thomas Hardy's England" (1984), collected in *Wormholes: Essays and Occasional Writings*, ed. Jan Relf (New York: Holt, 1998), 224; 1:254–55.
3. 2:170–78.
4. 1:696–99.
5. 4:248.
6. 5:479–81.

7. 5:524–28.

8. 5:501, 512–18.

9. 5:503–5.

Chapter 3: Wild Invention

Epigraph: 4:340–42.

1. 2:988–89, 1002–7.

2. 4:348–49.

3. 1:192–209.

4. Samuel Johnson, *The Lives of the Poets* (1781), quoted in Walter Jackson Bate, *Samuel Johnson* (New York: Harcourt Brace Jovanovich, 1977), 535.

5. 3:451–54.

6. 4:333–34, 343–47.

7. 4:332, 343, 321–22.

8. 4:618–22.

9. 4:396–408.

10. 4:410.

11. 4:429, 433–34.

Chapter 4: The Undefiled Bed

Epigraph: 4:750–52.

1. 4:736–41.

2. 4:740, 288–93.

3. 2:746, 762–67.

4. 4:761.

5. 4:492, 748–49; 2:777–87, 795.

6. 4:773–74.

7. 4:750, 5:15.

8. 4:300–301, 306–8.

9. 4:763–73.

10. 4:760.

Chapter 5: Gardening

Epigraph: 5:192–94.

1. 5:185–91.

2. 4:623–26, 627–32.

3. John Milton, *A Mask Presented at Ludlow Castle [Comus]* (1637), in Richard Aldington, ed., *The Viking Book of Poetry of the English-Speaking World* (New York: Viking, 1958), 398–99.

4. 4:438–39, 618, 243.

5. 4:262, 237–38; 5:206; 4:325–31.

6. 4:252–56.

7. Fedco seed catalog (Waterville, Maine, 2007), 55, 63.

8. 4:154–55.

9. 4:258–60.

10. 4:396, 347–50.

11. 4:800–804.

12. 4:622.

13. 4:633.

Chapter 6: Angels, Obedience, and ATVs

Epigraph: 6:373–76.

1. 5:277–87.

2. 6:16–18, 93–94, 96, 44–52.

3. 5:486.

4. 5:632–33, 640–41.

5. 5:308–11, 409–15.

6. 6:35–36, 3:372–74.

7. George Eliot, *Adam Bede* (1859), ed. Stephen Gill (London: Penguin, 1980), 67.

8. 5:882–87.

9. 5:529–30.

10. 1:26.

11. 4:62–63.

12. Eliot, *Adam Bede*, 69.

13. 3:648–50, 646, 624–29.

14. 6:113, 121, 121–26.

15. 6:164–69, 171, 174–81.

16. 5:650–53.

Chapter 7: Clear-Cuts

Epigraph: 6:584–89.

1. Hardy, "The Dorsetshire Laborer," 225; 4:207–8.

2. 6:509–15.

3. 6:784, 511, 503–4, 516.

4. 6:571–78.

5. 7:324.

6. Hardy, "The Dorsetshire Laborer," 225.

7. 7:235–42.

8. Lewis Carroll, *Alice's Adventures in Wonderland* (1865), in *The Annotated Alice*, ed. Martin Gardner (New York: Meridian, 1960), 25.

9. 6:637–46.

10. 6:646–55.

11. 6:667–78, 664–65, 542, 589–94.

12. 6:668–69.

13. 6:669–78.

14. 6:667, 669–70, 672.

15. 6:676, 781–74.

16. 6:829, 832, 833–34, 856–66.

17. 6:893–96.

18. 6:874–75, 889–92.

19. 6:901–2.

Chapter 8: The Mystery of Sons

Epigraph: 5:603–5.

1. 3:274–76.

2. 7:163–73.

3. "Rosemary," in *Italian Folk Tales*, retold by Italo Calvino, trans. George Martin (New York: Pantheon, 1980), 583–85.

4. 3:62–64.

5. 2:795–808.

6. 5:606–8.

7. 5:609–17.

8. "A Chronology of the Main Events of Milton's Life," in Milton, *Paradise Lost*, ix.

9. 1:26; 6:680, 723, 726–36.

10. 7:12–15.

11. 7:163–67.

12. 3:241.

13. 3:236–40.

14. 3:227–31.

Chapter 9: "Celestial Song"

Epigraph: 7:320–23.

1. 9:77–78, 55–57.

2. 8:359–63; 7:523; 9:476–77, 965; 7:323.

3. 7:417–20.

4. 1:13–16; 9:6, 30.

5. 7:463–73.

6. 9:24.

7. 7:421–22, 423–32.

8. 8:80–81.

9. 9:39–44.

10. 4:801–9.

11. 7:5, 7, 9–12.

12. 8:49–50, 44; 7:12–20.

13. 7:24, 24–25, 30–33, 38.

Chapter 10: "What Harmony or True Delight?"

Epigraph: 8:280–82.

1. 12:548, 351.

2. 8:267–71.

3. 8:271, 12:56; John Milton, Prolusion III (circa 1628–29), quoted in Lewalski, *Life*, 33.

4. 12:235–36, 469–78.

5. 12:518–19, 8:357–60.

6. John Milton, letter to Charles Diodati, 23 November 1637, quoted in Lewalski, *Life*, 70.

7. 8:381–84.

8. 8:571–74.

9. John Milton, *De Doctrina Christiana* (undated but probably finished by the mid-1660s), quoted in Christopher Hill, *Milton and the English Revolution* (London: Penguin, 1979), 136. See Lewalski, *Life*, 398, for speculation on dates.

10. 8:418–19; Christopher Milton, deposition on John Milton's will, 5 December 1674, quoted in Lewalski, *Life*, 387; 8:562–66. (Thanks to my mother, Janice Miller Potter, for unearthing this gem of crankiness.)

11. 8:409.

12. 11:268–84, 287–92.

13. John Milton, "On His Dead Wife" (1658), in John Frederick Nims, ed., *Western Wind: An Introduction to Poetry*, 2d ed. (New York: Random House, 1983), 427.

14. 8:600–602; Anne Bradstreet, "To My Dear and Loving Husband" (1678), in Nims, *Western Wind*, 427.

15. 1:12.

16. 8:538–46; John Aubrey, "John Milton," in *Brief Lives* (circa 1679–80), ed. Richard Barber (London: Folio Society, 1975), 208.

17. 12:576–87.

18. 8:589–92, 578.

Chapter 11: Killing Ruthie

Epigraph: 9:447–51.

1. 9:549; Wisława Szymborska, "The Terrorist, He's Watching" (1976), in *View with a Grain of Sand*, trans. Stanisław Barańczak and Clare Cavanagh (San Diego: Harcourt Brace, 1995), 108–9.

2. 9:459–66.

3. 9:473–79.

4. 5:596; 9:485, 487–88, 492, 718–30.

5. 9:510–22.

6. 9:614, 527–31.

7. 9:533, 607, 612, 550, 540, 547–48, 553–57.

8. 9:561, 570–71, 564–65.

9. 9:562, 563, 554.

10. 9:572–74, 558–59.

11. 9:575–83.

12. 9:588, 584, 589–93.

13. 9:588, 592, 594–97.

14. 9:617–20.

15. 9:626–30.

16. 9:786–92.

Chapter 12: Dust

Epigraph: 10:201–8.

1. 12:648.

2. 10:354–56.

3. 10:358–59, 356, 371, 348, 359.

4. 10:364, 469–72.

5. 10:480–83.

6. John Milton, *Ad Patrem* (undated but probably written in the 1630s); *An Apology against a Pamphlet Call'd A Modest Confutation of the Animadversions upon the Remonstrant against Smectymnuus* (1642); *Animadversions upon the Remonstrants Defence, Against Smectymnuus* (1641), all quoted in Lewalski, *Life*, 73, 137, 132; see 568, n. 79, for speculations on *Ad Patrem*'s date.

7. 10:500–501, 326–27.

8. 9:1080–90.

9. 10:501–3.

10. 10:504–16.

Afterword

Epigraph: John Keats, *Selected Poems and Letters*, ed. Douglas Bush (Boston: Houghton Mifflin, 1959), 131.

1. John Keats, letter to George Keats, 19 March 1819, quoted in Walter Jackson Bate, *John Keats* (Cambridge, Mass.: Harvard University Press, 1963), 476.

2. 1:13, 12:553–55.

3. 1:22–23.

About the Author

DAWN POTTER is the author of two poetry collections, most recently *How the Crimes Happened* (CavanKerry Press, 2010). She is associate director of the Frost Place Conference on Poetry and Teaching and lives in Harmony, Maine, with photographer Thomas Birtwistle and their two sons.